FIRST NATIONS HOCKEY PLAYERS

FIRST NATIONS HOCKEY PLAYERS

WILL CARDINAL

ESCHIA
BOOKS

The Publisher: Eschia Books Inc.

Library and Archives Canada Cataloguing in Publication

Cardinal, Will, 1962–
First Nations hockey players / by Will Cardinal.

Includes bibliographical references.
ISBN 978-0-9810942-1-2

1. Native hockey players—Canada—Biography. 2. National
Hockey League—Biography.
3. Native hockey players—Canada—History. I. Title.

GV848.5.A1C37 2009   796.962092'397071   C2008-907876-4

Project Director:
Kathy van Denderen
Cover Image:
Photos.com

PC: 5

You see other Native people being successful at something you are trying to be successful at, and you identify with that. It's definitely people you look up to, people whose footsteps you want to follow in. They were the leaders and the pioneers in the sport, the way I see it. It's nice to have role models like that.

–Sheldon Souray, Edmonton Oilers defenseman

Contents

A Short History of Native Hockey

What is a national sport? It is a sport that rises out of the substance of a nation, out of its soil and climate. To play hockey is constantly to repeat that men have transformed motionless winter, the hard earth, and suspended life, and that precisely out of all this they have made a swift, vigorous, passionate sport.

–Roland Barthes

TRACING THE HISTORY of a particular sport is like plotting your family tree. The further you go back in time, the larger the tree. Hockey's history is much like that of a family's, and the game's origins can be traced up many branches. While the actual birthplace of hockey will continue to be debated by historians for years to come, it is clear that the game did not spring up overnight. One of the game's biggest influences came from the various tribes throughout North America who played a game similar to what we recognize as hockey.

With the long winters and plenty of ice, the tribes of the north had many winter games, but their version of "ice hockey" was one of the most popular. "Ice shinny," as it is most commonly referred to, was popular among the Sioux, Crow, Blackfoot and numerous other tribes of Canada. Although each tribe had slightly different rules, the core of the game remained constant. Playing on a rectangular ice surface, the teams consisted of between 10 and 50 players per team. The object of the game was to hit the "puck," usually a piece of wood or stone covered with rawhide, into the opponent's goal. The goal was marked with two logs or branches stuck in the ice. The only difference to today's hockey nets is that the posts were placed anywhere from 10 to 20 feet apart.

Although the players had sticks and a puck and played on ice, that is where the technical similarities with the modern game of hockey end, but shinny was still just as fast paced and violent as the hockey played today. The game was played for fun or in fierce competition between rival tribes as a way of settling disputes, with no loss of life but with plenty of lost teeth.

When European settlers began arriving in the 16th century on the eastern coast of Canada, they noticed that the Mi'kmaq Indians played a game on ice with sticks and a "puck." Similar to the game of bandy, a European stick-and-ball game played on ice, the Mi'kmaq game and the European version can definitely be cited as the precursors to the modern game of hockey.

But the Native influence on hockey's history does not end with the arrival of the Europeans. First Nation hockey players, from the minor leagues through to the NHL, have always been at the forefront of the game, battling hard to get the respect they deserve and leaving an impression of success for future generations to come.

PART I

Current Players

Aaron
Asham

BORN IN PORTAGE LA PRAIRIE, Manitoba, in 1978 to proud Métis parents, Aaron Asham got his start in professional hockey with the Red Deer Rebels of the Western Hockey League. A gifted goal scorer in his junior days, he was drafted 71st overall by the Montreal Canadiens in 1996.

It was the Canadiens' hope that the kid who had scored 43 goals in his last year with the Rebels in 1997–98 would do the same for them, but Asham seemed to fit in better on the checking line. However, the Canadiens were never fully satisfied with the energetic forward and regularly sent him down to the minors.

Knowing that he could contribute more to a team, Asham was happy to find out that he was being traded to the New York Islanders in 2002.

It would be a chance to prove himself, and the Islanders needed his skill set on the team. In his first year on the Isle, Asham had his most productive season, scoring 15 goals and 19 assists. He played four, full, productive seasons with the Islanders before being traded to the New Jersey Devils in 2007.

Asham played in 77 games during his first season with the Devils and was a regular contributor to the special teams (the lines specializing in the power play and penalty kill). But one year later he opted to sign with the Philadelphia Flyers, a team that needed a boost in defensive skills. Asham is currently a regular on the team's third and fourth lines and is becoming a defensive specialist.

Stats

Season	Team	Games Played	Goals	Assists	Points	Penalties
1998–99	Montreal Canadiens	7	0	0	0	0
1999–2000	Montreal Canadiens	33	4	2	6	24
2000–01	Montreal Canadiens	46	2	3	5	59
2001–02	Montreal Canadiens	35	5	4	9	55
2002–03	New York Islanders	78	15	19	34	57
2003–04	New York Islanders	79	12	12	24	92
2005–06	New York Islanders	63	9	15	24	103
2006–07	New York Islanders	80	11	12	23	63
2007–08	New Jersey Devils	77	6	4	10	84
NHL Totals		498	64	71	135	537

Rene
Bourque

BORN IN LAC LA BICHE, Alberta, Rene Bourque was always aware of his Métis heritage. And like many kids his age, hockey was a fixture in his life, and the young Bourque took to the game quite naturally.

In 1999–2000 he joined the St. Albert Saints of the Alberta Junior Hockey League and was one of the team's top-scoring left wings, potting 44 goals in 63 games. Looking for a greater challenge to his hockey career, Bourque packed his bags and moved to the University of Wisconsin to join the Badgers. Many an NHL player had come up through the team's ranks, including Stanley Cup winner and Norris Trophy defenseman Chris Chelios, so Bourque thought the training and the education would be the perfect route to take on his path to the NHL.

He enjoyed mediocre success in Wisconsin, but after graduating he moved on to the Norfolk Admirals of the American Hockey League and scored a franchise record 33 goals. He was then signed to an entry-level contract by the Chicago Blackhawks and made his first NHL appearance in the 2005–06 season. His route to the NHL was a little different from most, having never been drafted, but he'd made it, and that was all that mattered.

In his first season with the Hawks, he received full confidence from the coaching staff and put in a respectable performance, scoring 16 goals. He was proving to be a reliable forward who was always responsible on the defensive end of the game. But it was that defensive mindset that nearly got him killed in the 2006–07 season.

During a game in November 2006 against the Columbus Blue Jackets, a pile-up occurred in front of the Blackhawk net, and while Bourque was lying on the ground trying to cover up the puck, Blue Jacket forward Nikolai Zherdev accidentally stepped on his neck with his skate. Blood poured onto the ice as trainers rushed off the bench to Bourque's side. He was rushed to the hospital where doctors repaired the damage to his neck and saved his life. The blade had cut through the muscle in his neck and gouged his jugular vein, coming close to ending his life. He returned to play that season but was not effective.

After playing another season with the Hawks in 2007–08, he was traded to his current team, the Calgary Flames, during the off-season. If he can remain healthy, Bourque will be a player to watch in the future.

Stats

Season	Team	Games Played	Goals	Assists	Points	Penalties
2005–06	Chicago Blackhawks	77	16	18	34	56
2006–07	Chicago Blackhawks	44	7	10	17	38
2007–08	Chicago Blackhawks	62	10	14	24	42
NHL Totals		183	33	42	75	136

Jonathan Cheechoo

AS A MEMBER OF THE Moose Cree First Nation, Jonathan Cheechoo knows that a lot of people are proud of him and how far he has come. Born in 1980 in the small town of Moose Factory, Ontario, Jonathan fell in love with hockey early on. Never a fast skater, he made up for his lack of speed with an incredible sense for the game and lightning-fast hands.

Those skills got him noticed, and in 1997 he joined the Belleville Bulls of the Ontario Hockey League. Although he scored 31 goals, then 35, then 45, in his first three years in juniors, hockey scouts were wary of the talented forward because of his slow skating.

At the time of the 1998 NHL Entry Draft, many teams were looking at Cheechoo, as most knew him to have natural scoring talent, but to be an NHL player you had to be able to skate fast, and Cheechoo was not much of a skater compared with the other draft selections. When the draft started, his stock seemed to continue to fall until the San Jose Sharks decided to take a chance on him and selected him 29th overall. The Sharks saw something in Cheechoo and made him their top priority. After spending some time in the American Hockey League, Cheechoo finally got the call to play for the Sharks in the 2002–03 season. He was lucky to get to play in 66 games, but he only managed to score nine goals.

Unhappy with his performance, Cheechoo worked out heavily during the off-season, putting himself through a grueling power-skating regime and built his upper body strength. The work paid off. When he rejoined the Sharks for the 2003–04 season, he scored 28 goals in 81 games. He went from a fourth-line defensive player to the Sharks' top line scoring forward in one season and hasn't left that spot since.

But as good as his 2003–04 season was, Cheechoo shone when the NHL returned from the lockout in 2005–06. Teamed up with former Boston Bruin Joe Thornton, Cheechoo won the goal-scoring race, potting 56 goals and winning the coveted Maurice

Richard Trophy, awarded to the player who scores the most goals in one season.

His production dropped off in 2006–07 to 37 goals, but the Sharks know that they have a player who will continue to produce for them well into the future, which is why they signed him to a five-year contract extension in 2006 worth $15 million.

As the Sharks move forward, Cheechoo hopes that he can help his team move toward the ultimate goal of winning the Stanley Cup.

Stats

Season	Team	Games Played	Goals	Assists	Points	Penalties
2002–03	San Jose Sharks	66	9	7	16	39
2003–04	San Jose Sharks	81	28	19	47	33
2005–06	San Jose Sharks	82	56	37	93	58
2006–07	San Jose Sharks	76	37	32	69	69
2007–08	San Jose Sharks	69	23	14	37	46
NHL Totals		374	153	109	262	245

Vernon Fiddler

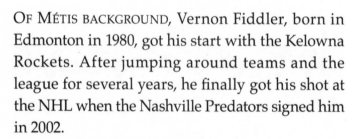

OF MÉTIS BACKGROUND, Vernon Fiddler, born in Edmonton in 1980, got his start with the Kelowna Rockets. After jumping around teams and the league for several years, he finally got his shot at the NHL when the Nashville Predators signed him in 2002.

He played only a few games a season for the Predators until 2006–07, when he played a full 72 games, scoring 11 goals. Not a natural goal scorer, the big center is a defensive-minded player who is often used on the Predators' special teams. His hard work throughout his hockey career has finally paid off with a full-time position in the Predators organization.

Stats

Season	Team	Games Played	Goals	Assists	Points	Penalties
2002–03	Nashville Predators	19	4	2	6	14
2003–04	Nashville Predators	17	0	0	0	23
2005–06	Nashville Predators	40	8	4	12	42
2006–07	Nashville Predators	72	11	15	26	40
2007–08	Nashville Predators	79	11	21	32	47
NHL Totals		227	34	42	76	166

Carey
Price

ONE OF THE MOST TALKED ABOUT and highly touted
First Nations hockey players to enter the NHL in
a long time, Carey Price got his start in Vancouver,
British Columbia. Born to a white father and an
Ulkatcho First Nation mother, young Price wanted
to be just like his father, a goalie who was drafted
by the Philadelphia Flyers 126th overall in the 1978
Amateur Draft. His father never played in the
NHL, but he did pass on everything he learned to
his young son, and the extra advice paid off.

But growing up in the remote area of Anahi Lake
in BC provided a unique challenge to getting young
Carey to his hockey games. It took too long for his
parents to drive young Price to hockey, so Carey's
father bought himself a plane, and every time
Carey had to play, his father would start up his

plane and fly him first class to his games. It was an expensive method of travel, but the sacrifice paid off when Carey started showing potential and was signed to the Tri-City Americans of the Western Hockey League.

Tri-City wasn't the best team, but they were made competitive by having Price in nets. He posted an average of under 3.00 goals-against in his five years with the team and proved he could play under intense pressure. In 2005, Montreal Canadiens general manager Bob Gainey recognized the potential in the young goaltender and used the fifth pick overall to select Price at the NHL Entry Draft.

After spending one more year with the Tri-City team, Price moved to the Canadiens' farm team, the Hamilton Bulldogs of the American Hockey League, in 2006 and led the team to the Calder Cup. That same year he was the goaltender for the Canadian Junior National team, who went on to win the gold medal. For his amazing goaltending during the tournament he was named the Most Valuable Player, the top goaltender of the tournament and named to the All-Star team. He also won the Canadian Hockey League's 2006–07 Goaltender of the Year and the Jack Butterfield Trophy as the Calder Cup MVP.

With stats like those, the Montreal Canadiens could not keep Price down on the farm too long and called him up on October 10, 2007, in a game against the Pittsburgh Penguins. He made 26 saves in a 3–2 victory to record his first NHL win. After playing with the Canadiens until January 2008, he was sent back down to Hamilton for reconditioning but was recalled just one month later.

Price was permanently handed the job of the Canadiens' number-one goaltender when Cristobal Huet was traded to the Washington Capitals. Price proved to the management that they had made a good decision when he led the team through to the end of the season finishing first in the Eastern Conference. He backstopped the Canadiens to a hard-fought win over the Boston Bruins in the first round of the playoffs, but he looked shaky in a five-game series loss to the Philadelphia Flyers. Price suggested that he was simply exhausted by then, after having played hockey for nearly two straight years, moving from Hamilton to the Calder Cup then to the World Juniors and onto the Canadiens.

After taking the summer off and spending some time with his family, Price returned to the Canadiens 25 pounds lighter and ready for a new season. He and goaltender Jaroslav Halak have led the Canadiens off to a good start at the beginning of the 2008–09 season, and they hope to make the Canadiens' 100th year in the NHL a memorable one. Price will definitely be a player to watch in the future and a member of the First Nations to be proud of.

Stats

Season	Team	Games Played	Minutes Played	Goals Against	Shut out	Goals Against Average	Wins	Losses	Over-time Losses
2007–08	Montreal Canadiens	41	2413	103	3	2.56	24	12	3
NHL Totals		41	2413	103	3	2.56	24	12	3

D.J. King

BORN IN MEADOW LAKE, Saskatchewan, D.J. King, a Métis, has taken the long route to the NHL. Starting off in the Western Hockey League with the Lethbridge Hurricanes, King became known as a tough player not shy to drop the gloves. In 2002 he was drafted 190th overall by the St. Louis Blues but never really got his chance to break in the NHL. He spent the next several years jumping around the American Hockey League before the St. Louis Blues finally gave him a chance in 2006 and added him to their lineup. He played his first full season with the Blues in 2007–08, scoring only three goals in 61 games. As of this writing, he currently remains with the Blues organization.

Stats

Season	Team	Games Played	Goals	Assists	Points	Penalties
2006–07	St. Louis Blues	27	1	1	2	52
2007–08	St. Louis Blues	61	3	3	6	100
NHL Totals		88	4	4	8	152

Sheldon
Souray

A Métis from Elk River, Alberta, Sheldon Souray was not an immediate success when he first broke into the NHL. In fact, it took him a long time just to get his skates onto NHL ice.

Drafted by the New Jersey Devils in 1994, Souray did not play his first NHL game until 1997. Now, he is known for his scoring abilities, but when the 6-foot 4-inch defenseman first entered the league, he only tallied three goals. That is not to say that Souray wasn't useful to the team. With his long reach and imposing physique, he was perfect on the Devils blue line, but he always knew he had more to give. In 1999 he was traded mid-season to the Montreal Canadiens, and it was there that he began to turn his career around to become the star we know today.

He played well in his first few seasons with the Canadiens but spent most of his time on the injured reserved list. He played only 52 games in 2000–01, 34 games the following season and did not play at all in 2002–03. When he returned to action in 2003–04 fully recovered, the Canadiens management, who had noticed Souray's powerful slapshot during practice, decided to put him on the point during the power play, and the gamble paid off. Souray scored 15 goals that year, and in 2006–07 he increased that total to 26. He had achieved the level of superstar, even making the All-Star team that year.

When Souray hit free agency that season, he decided to test the market to see who wanted his services. Many teams came calling, but one team in particular caught his attention. Being from the Edmonton area, Souray was more than happy to sign a $27-million contract with the Oilers for a five-year term. Many had figured that he would move to Los Angeles, given that his ex-wife (model Angie Everheart) and child lived there, but Souray's heart was always close to home, and playing in Edmonton gave him a chance to be close to his family and old friends.

> "I'm from Fisher Lake, a Métis settlement in Alberta, but I was born in Elk River, which is the closest village to our community. I moved away from our settlement to

play in Edmonton, and the family moved. But all my uncles, my grandma and family are still in Fisher Lake. More than anything, growing up in Alberta, with the Oilers winning all those Stanley Cups with Wayne Gretzky, and everybody else, I always wanted to be an Oiler, pure and simple as that."

But Souray's introduction to Edmonton took on a sour note when, a few games into the season, he was injured and forced to watch games from the press box. It was a tough pill for such a proud man to swallow, but he has returned for a new season, bent on proving to the people of Edmonton that he can be the player they want.

"As for Native role models who impacted on me growing up, I was able to identify with Fred Sasakamoose and Reggie Leach through my experience with the Aboriginal Role Model Hockey School. You see other Native people being successful at something you are trying to be successful at, and you identify with that. They are definitely people you look up to, people whose footsteps you want to follow in. They were the leaders and the pioneers in the sport, the way I see it. It's nice to have role models like that," said Souray in the book *They Call Me Chief.* Souray is now one of those role models that Native kids look up to, believing that they too can achieve what he has, not just in the NHL but in life as well.

Stats

Season	Team	Games Played	Goals	Assists	Points	Penalties
1997–98	New Jersey Devils	60	3	7	10	85
1998–99	New Jersey Devils	70	1	7	8	110
1999–2000	New Jersey Devils	52	0	8	8	70
	Montreal Canadiens	19	3	0	3	44
2000–01	Montreal Canadiens	52	3	8	11	95
2001–02	Montreal Canadiens	34	3	5	8	62
2003–04	Montreal Canadiens	63	15	20	35	104
2005–06	Montreal Canadiens	75	12	27	39	116
2006–07	Montreal Canadiens	81	26	38	64	135
2007–08	Edmonton Oilers	26	3	7	10	36
NHL Totals		532	69	127	196	857

Jordin Tootoo

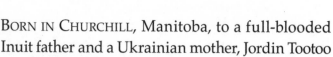

BORN IN CHURCHILL, Manitoba, to a full-blooded Inuit father and a Ukrainian mother, Jordin Tootoo actually grew up in Rankin Inlet, Nunavut. Growing up in Nunavut allowed him to be close to his father's culture and to learn the traditional ways of his people. Living in the north also gave him plenty of access to ice, and when young Jordin was first introduced to the game he took to it immediately.

As he grew up he realized that he could not remain in the north if he wanted to pursue a career in hockey. He had to go south, and in 1999 he joined the Brandon Wheat Kings of the Western Hockey League. It was there that he established the style of play that he would become well known for in years to come.

At 5 feet 9 inches, Tootoo was not the biggest player on the ice, but he more than made up for that in toughness. In his first year with the Wheat Kings he amassed 214 minutes in penalties in just 45 games and only scored six goals.

The following year Tootoo calmed down a little and focused more on his game and improved to 20 goals and 172 minutes in penalties in 60 games. The rough edge to his game, his incredible speed on the ice and his ability to score goals caught the attention of the Nashville Predators at the 2001 NHL Entry Draft. He was selected 98th overall and two years later got his chance at the NHL level.

Simply making it to the NHL was an incredible feat for Tootoo. In doing so he became the first Inuit to ever be drafted and the first to play in the NHL. Even before he played his first game with Nashville he was already a hero to many. He only scored four goals in his first year with the Predators, but his physical style and energy kept him on the team.

Most often used as a fourth-line forward, Tootoo has become quite good at bothering opposing players, but that skill has gotten him into some trouble with the league over the years. Most notably was the incident when he sucker punched Dallas Stars defenseman Stephane Robidas in the face during a March 2007 game, sending Robidas to the hospital with a concussion. The media, and especially

Don Cherry, were upset over the incident, and Tootoo was labeled a few times as being a cheap-shot artist. The theory seemed to hold true when he knocked out Phoenix Coyotes player Daniel Winnik with a shoulder shot to the head later that year.

Tootoo has claimed that none of the incidents were done on purpose and that he just plays the game in a physical manner and that sometimes his energetic style can get the better of him. There is little doubt he will change that style, since it was what had got him into the NHL in the first place and why so many fans love him. Today, Tootoo remains a fixture in the Nashville Predators lineup and probably an NHL player for many years to come.

Stats

Season	Team	Games Played	Goals	Assists	Points	Penalties
2003–04	Nashville Predators	70	4	4	8	137
2005–06	Nashville Predators	34	4	6	10	55
2006–07	Nashville Predators	65	3	6	9	116
2007–08	Nashville Predators	63	11	7	18	100
NHL Totals		232	22	23	45	408

PART II

Legends

Fred
Sasakamoose

WHILE HE HAS THE DISTINCTION of being the first
Native hockey player to break the National Hockey
League (NHL) barrier, Fred Sasakamoose did not
have a long or fruitful professional hockey career.
What makes his story so compelling is the struggle
he had to endure just to get his foot in the door and
the legacy he left in his community.

The official record books state that Sasakamoose
played 11 games in the NHL for the Chicago Blackhawks, had zero goals, zero assists and six minutes
in penalties. His record may seem to be a minor
blip on the radar screen of hockey statistical history,
but what the numbers do not reveal is what his
accomplishment meant to the history of the NHL
and to all First Nations peoples. Sasakamoose
opened the door for generations of young Native

men to follow in his footsteps and add to the history of the NHL. Without his efforts, the long line of great Native hockey players such as George Armstrong, Bryan Trottier, Theoren Fleury and Carey Price may never have been possible.

Growing up on the Big River Reserve in Saskatchewan in the 1930s and '40s, Fred Sasakamoose did not have much as a child growing up. While many young boys his age began to discover hockey, with parents who bought them a pair of skates and a hockey stick, Sasakamoose grew up with little and had to resort to using tree branches for a stick and rocks for a puck.

Sasakamoose's upbringing was like many other Native kids during that time. Taken away from his parents at the age of five by the government, he was placed in an Indian residential school. The aim was to give the Native children a chance at an education that they never would have received on a reserve, but what actually went on in those "schools" was far from a normal education.

Although Sasakamoose did not have it as hard as some Native children during that time, life in the school was not ideal. He was not allowed to speak his Cree language or to observe any cultural practices. Punishment for disobeying the rules was severe, and after morning classes the children were sent to work on the school's farm.

However, despite all the work, there was still time to be a kid, and in the winter the only way to do that was to play hockey. The priests at the school were all from Montreal and therefore loved their hockey. Seven days a week the priests coached those boys the same way they taught them in school, and all the extra discipline began to show in Sasakamoose's game, as he quickly became the best hockey player in the school. The entire school benefited from the extra work, and by the time he was 14 years old, Sasakamoose's team had won the Northern Saskatchewan Midget hockey championship in 1946, the first Native school to win the title.

Sasakamoose's skills on the ice got him noticed, and the Moose Jaw Canucks of the Western Hockey League soon came calling and signed him to their team for the start of the 1950–51 season. It wasn't easy to go from the small-town life of the reserve to a "white" city like Moose Jaw. There were racist comments all the time, but Sasakamoose just put his head down and tried to let his game speak for itself. By his second season in Moose Jaw, most of the hockey fans had quieted down with their inappropriate comments because Sasakamoose was by then one of the best players on the ice—so much so that the head coach nominated him as captain of the team. In his second year with the team,

Sasakamoose become the power center of the team, scoring 19 goals and 22 assists in 42 games.

When he was 16 years old, the Chicago Blackhawks had already recognized the talent in Sasakamoose and had him sign a letter for $100, committing himself to the franchise when he came of age. At 20 years old, Sasakamoose finally got that call.

"You have a dream. A dream to play in the NHL—couldn't go any higher. The Chicago Blackhawks got a hold of me. They said, 'You report to Toronto on Saturday night.' Being a Native in this world is very hard. I realized my dream: the NHL," said Sasakamoose in an interview with Don Marks from his book *They Call Me Chief.*

The transition from the small-town Indian reserve to the skyscrapers of Toronto was a shock at first, but even more so was getting to meet legendary radio broadcaster Foster Hewitt. Sasakamoose had grown up listening to Hewitt's broadcast every Saturday night and could not believe he was getting the chance to talk to him. But the meeting did not go as Sasakamoose had imagined. Speaking to Hewitt over the telephone, after dispensing with the usual greetings, Sasakamoose was asked how to pronounce his name, "Sasaketchwan-moose, Saskatoon-moose," said Hewitt in a condescending manner, to which Sasakamoose simply hung up the phone. It was a bold move for an NHL rookie to make, but Sasakamoose had his pride.

What was most notable about Fred Sasakamoose during his short stay in the NHL was that he was a hard worker and a deceptively fast skater, and he had one of the hardest slapshots in the NHL. But life in the big city proved to be too much for the kid from small-town Saskatchewan. If the hustle of Moose Jaw had bothered him at first, imagine what the bright lights and fast pace life of Chicago would do to a kid who grew up in a log cabin. He wanted to be near his family and his young wife. He played with the Blackhawks for the last 11 games of the 1953–54 season and returned home during the off-season.

Yet when it came time for him to return to camp, Sasakamoose just didn't have what it took to survive away from his land and people, and he left the bright lights of the NHL for the Calgary Stampeders of the Western Hockey League. But even Calgary was too far from home for his liking, especially for his wife, so he hung up his skates.

But he never stayed completely away from the game; after all, to his people he was like Maurice Richard. He continued to play recreational games and established hockey schools to give Native youths a direction.

His time playing in the NHL might have been brief, but Fred Sasakamoose's impact on the game and for the history of his people was legendary.

Stats

Season	Team	Games Played	Goals	Assists	Points	Penalties
1953–54	Chicago Blackhawks	11	0	0	0	6
NHL Totals		11	0	0	0	6

Reggie Leach

TO SAY THAT REGGIE LEACH came from humble beginnings would be an understatement. Born to unmarried teenage parents in Riverton, Manitoba, in 1950, Leach, a Métis, grew up in the care of his grandparents in a house with 12 other children. There was hardly any money, and the pall of alcoholism always hung over the household. The story is all too familiar in some Native communities across North America, and many children with enormous potential often get caught in the middle. While Leach watched many around him sinking further into despair, he managed to find an outlet for his frustrations and a possible way out of a life he never wanted.

"My grandparents didn't have the money to pay for ice time at the local indoor arena. It was 25 cents an hour or $2.50 for the season. So I skated around on the outdoor rink. It was cold, and sometimes lonely, but a 10-year-old kid is never really alone because, in your imagination, you're playing on some NHL team against another NHL team for the Stanley Cup," said Leach.

Leach never did well in school, but on the ice he was turning out to be an "A" student. Hockey was his one escape from a life of poverty, and he put his heart and soul into the game. When he was just 13, he was recruited to play in a local semi-pro club with guys who were 10 to 15 years older than him.

As promising as his on-ice career seemed to be, in his mid to late teens Leach still fell victim to the bottle. Several times a week he would drink to the point of getting really drunk, and a few times he played while intoxicated. Even while fighting off the hangovers, he played hockey better than most in his area, but he was still in danger of becoming another Native statistic. His drinking got to the point that his coach Sigg John began to notice it was affecting his game. John took it upon himself to sit the young Leach down and have a serious talk with him about the path in life he was taking.

One afternoon, coach and player sat down at restaurant across from the local bar. John pointed in the direction of two Native men who were known to be the town drunks. He told Leach that they had once been promising hockey players, but they had chosen the bottle over hockey. Seeing the two men woke Leach to the possibility that he too could be led down that road. The talk seemed to have had an impact on Leach, at least for the time being.

With his hockey career and life back on track, Leach joined forces with the Flin Flon Bombers for the 1966–67 season. It was in Flin Flon that he was partnered up with future NHL linemate Bobby Clarke.

Together Clarke and Leach became an unstoppable force. In his first season, Leach scored an incredible 67 goals, and in the following season potted an even more incredible 87 goals. It goes without saying that he made the All-Star team each year and was a favorite of local rabid hockey fans. There was little entertainment in such a small town, and hockey was about the only escape people had in the dead of winter. The town was split clearly between the whites and the Native population, but when it came to hockey, everyone could agree, and Leach and Clarke were the town's two poster boys for unity.

After two more successful seasons with the Bombers, it was just a matter of time before the NHL came calling to pluck this talent out of the obscurity of Flin Flon. At the 1970 NHL Amateur Draft, the Boston Bruins used their number-one pick to select Leach third overall behind Gilbert Perreault (Buffalo) and Dale Talon (Vancouver).

But the signing did not do much for the pursuit of Leach's NHL career. He had the misfortune to sign with the Bruins one year after they had won the Cup, and in those days teams did not change much from the winning combination.

Leach got to play in 23 games during the 1970–71 season and was in awe of getting to skate beside the likes of Bobby Orr and Phil Esposito, but he felt he wasn't being used to the best of his abilities. The following season he played in 56 games but received little ice time or encouragement from the coaching staff. Halfway through the season he was packaged off with other players and traded to the California Golden Seals, where his career finally started to turn around for the better.

In his first full season in the Sunshine State in 1972–73, he scored 23 goals in 76 games. In his second full season with the club he was promoted to the first line and was the team's "go to guy" on the power play. But for some reason, management felt that Leach had served his time with the club and that a bunch of fresh new faces were required to lift the Golden Seals out of the basement of the league. During the 1975 off-season, Leach was traded to the defending Stanley Cup Champion Philadelphia Flyers and was reunited with his old linemates from the minors, Bobby Clarke and Bill Barber.

In the beginning, it was not a happy reunion. Leach went the first quarter of the season with only three goals and was in danger of losing the cherished position next to Clarke. But after some encouragement from head coach Fred Shero and Clarke, Leach dramatically turned his season around.

Combined, the line became one of the top scoring units in the league. Leach scored 45 goals that year, and the sheer number of goals put in the net was instrumental in leading the Flyers back to their second straight Stanley Cup victory.

The 1975–76 season saw Leach improve even more. He scored a career-high 61 goals and led the Flyers into the playoffs with the second-best regular-season record behind the Montreal Canadiens. As good as he was in the regular season, Leach had an extra gear for the playoffs.

In the first round of the playoffs against the Toronto Maple Leafs, the Flyers probably would not have moved on if it weren't for Leach. Potting goals by the bunch, he helped the Flyers get past the tenacious Leafs, taking the series to seven games. It was a high-scoring series, but Leach simply put the Flyers over the top and helped out-score Toronto straight out of the playoffs and onto the golf course.

Leach continued his amazing play and helped the Flyers take out the Bruins in the semi-final round and propel them into the Stanley Cup finals for a shot at a third consecutive Stanley Cup. In the entire playoffs, Leach scored 19 goals, but it wasn't enough to get past the Canadiens. He established a record for most goals in the playoffs—a mark that has only been equaled by Jari Kurri of the Edmonton Oilers in the 1985 playoffs. Despite losing the Stanley Cup final in four straight to the Canadiens, Leach's record-setting performance of 19 goals earned him the Conn Smythe Trophy as the playoffs' most valuable player. He was the first hockey player of Native descent to win the trophy. (The New York Islanders Bryan Trottier became the second when he won it in 1980.)

Leach never again managed to produce another 60-goal season, as alcohol began to creep into his life once again. He would show up to practices drunk, and his play on the ice suffered. Yet, he somehow still managed to score an average of 30 goals per season. But he could have been so much more.

"Alcohol was available all the time in the NHL. It was in the dressing room, on the bus, on airplane flights. I played many games hung over," said Leach. "I would quit, but then I would start right back up again. Some years, I couldn't tell if my lower scoring totals were the result of stress trying to sober up, or because I was still drinking."

After an excellent season in 1979–80 when Leach scored 50 goals, the Flyers made it to the Stanley Cup finals again, but this time their opponent was the New York Islanders. This was the Islanders of Bryan Trottier and Billy Smith, and they made short work of the Flyers in six games.

That series was Leach's last shot at the Stanley Cup. He played two more seasons in Philadelphia before he was shipped off to Detroit, where he played out the 1982–83 season and scored only 15 goals. It was his last season in the NHL, as teams did not want to take a chance on a player who clearly had alcohol problems. Leach later admitted that he could have played several more years in the pros, but that alcohol ended his chances and took away his dream of making it into the Hockey Hall of Fame.

Just a year after retiring, Leach finally got the help he needed and quit drinking for good. And to make up for his mistakes, Reggie Leach traveled all across North America visiting Native communities to warn young people of the dangers of alcohol abuse. In 2007, he returned to the hockey world when he signed on as associate coach of the Manitoulin Islanders of the Northern Ontario Junior Hockey League, where he continues to inspire.

Stats

Season	Team	Games Played	Goals	Assists	Points	Penalties
1970–71	Boston Bruins	23	2	4	6	0
1971–72	Boston Bruins	56	7	13	20	12
	California Golden Seals	17	6	7	13	7
1972–73	California Golden Seals	76	23	12	35	45
1973–74	California Golden Seals	78	22	24	46	34
1974–75	Philadelphia Flyers	80	45	33	78	63
1975–76	Philadelphia Flyers	80	61	30	91	41
1976–77	Philadelphia Flyers	77	32	14	46	23
1977–78	Philadelphia Flyers	72	24	28	52	24
1978–79	Philadelphia Flyers	76	34	20	54	20
1979–80	Philadelphia Flyers	76	50	26	76	28
1980–81	Philadelphia Flyers	79	34	36	70	59
1981–82	Philadelphia Flyers	66	26	21	47	18
1982–83	Detroit Red Wings	78	15	17	32	13
NHL Totals		934	381	285	666	387

Stan
Jonathan

LIKE MANY NATIVE AMERICAN hockey players before him, when Stan Jonathan began playing hockey, he was given the extremely uncreative nickname of "Little Chief." It is a moniker that many Native players in sports are unfortunately saddled with. Some do not like it, while others just accept it. Jonathan accepted Little Chief, but that was as far as he would go.

"They called me Little Chief, and I didn't mind that. It was when they called me 'wahoo' or 'F@#$n' little Indian' that I didn't like," Jonathan said in an interview with Don Marks from a documentary called *They Call Me Chief.*

Growing up as a young man on the Six Nations Reserve near Brantford, Ontario, Jonathan learned that fierce pride in his Mohawk heritage from the proud people who surrounded him. When he began playing hockey, the pride and desire to succeed served him well throughout his career because, at 5 feet 8 inches and 175 pounds, Jonathan was often the smallest player on the ice.

Jonathan does not remember a specific time when he began playing hockey, because there always seemed to be a place and time for the game. With 14 brothers and sisters, Jonathan always had someone to play with, but as one of the youngest, he had to develop a tough skin. He moved into competitive hockey at the age of 11 and moved quickly through the ranks. By the time he reached his late teens, he was good enough to join the Peterborough Petes of the Ontario Junior A Hockey League in 1972.

In his junior days Jonathan was quite the prolific scorer, and although he protected himself on the ice, it wasn't a major part of his style. His energetic manner and physical play caught the eye of Hockey Canada, and Jonathan was invited to the unofficial, first World Junior Championship in Leningrad in 1973.

In each successive year in the junior ranks, Jonathan's scoring prowess improved steadily to the point that in his last year with the Petes in 1974–75, he scored 36 goals and 39 assists in 70 games.

With his success on the ice, Jonathan was becoming a role model in his community, but he was still just in his teens and was oblivious to this consideration. Plus he had more important things to look after—while he was in Junior A his future wife Cathy got pregnant. It was something he had to keep quiet because, as he says in the documentary interview, there were so few spots in the NHL, and any "character flaw" might keep him from his dream. Keeping a low profile was important to Jonathan, and his sacrifices paid off at the 1975 NHL Amateur Draft.

Looking to inject a little energy and spirit into their lineup, the Boston Bruins used their fourth pick to select Jonathan. He could not have found a better match in the NHL. Coached by the always outspoken Don Cherry, the Bruins were a talented scoring team surrounded by brute toughness. Terry O'Reilly and Mike Millbury were the resident tough guys, and by adding Jonathan, the Bruins hoped to match the physical play of teams such as the "Broad Street Bullies" (better known as the Philadelphia Flyers) and to add the extra bit of scoring power that he could provide. It was Cherry himself who made sure that Jonathan was selected by the Bruins. "I couldn't help but notice this rugged little Indian," said Cherry of the first time he saw Jonathan play.

> "He didn't play an exceptional game, but there was something about him that made

me take notice. Harry (Sinden, Bruins general manager) was not as impressed as I was, and bypassed Jonathan on the first, second, and third picks. We finally got him the fourth time around....Of all my discoveries, Jonathan is the one in which I take most pride."

Lofty words of praise for Jonathan from one of Canada's premiere figures in hockey.

Although he got to play in one game with the Bruins in the 1975–76 season, Jonathan was called up full time with the team in 1976–77 and instantly found favor with the club and the Bruins' fans. In his rookie season he potted a respectable 17 goals and 13 assists in 69 games and earned the confidence of his coach Don Cherry to play in all of the team's 14 playoff games. They made it all the way to the final against the Montreal Canadiens, only to lose in four straight. With the chance given to him by Cherry, Jonathan was not going to waste the opportunity, and he returned for the 1977–78 season with something to prove.

"I was just happy to be there. Being small, and being a Native, you had to get in there and show them that you weren't going to be pushed around. I always had more penalty minutes than I should have, but I was always there for the other players, too," said Jonathan.

And boy, could he fight. In his first tilt in the NHL he took on Chicago Blackhawks' tough guy Keith Magnuson and won quite easily. Other contenders included several of the toughest of the tough in the league at the time, including the Flyers' Dave "the Hammer" Schultz and Andre "Moose" Dupont. Jonathan was labeled a "tough guy," but he valued his contributions on the scoreboard much more.

His point totals were helped along by the fact that he played on the number-one line to the left of the Bruins' star player Jean Ratelle. As a young player in the NHL, Jonathan could not have asked for a better learning experience than in his first two years with the Bruins. For the second year in a row the Bruins made it into the playoffs, dispensed with their first two opponents and made it to the Stanley Cup final once again against the Montreal Canadiens. Unfortunately, history repeated itself, and the Canadiens again walked away with the Stanley Cup. This was an especially bitter pill to swallow, so during the off-season, as he did every year, Jonathan returned to his home near the reserve where he grew up to decompress.

The 1978–79 season was not kind to Jonathan; he missed the majority of the season because of an injury. But he did return in time for the playoffs, where he enjoyed probably the best moment of his career.

After easily dispensing of the Pittsburgh Penguins in the opening round of the 1979 playoffs, the Bruins moved on to the semi-finals to face their nemesis in what turned out to be one of the most memorable games in the two clubs' long and contemptuous history.

The Canadiens were without a doubt the best team of the late 1970s. They had a skilled defense, one of the greatest goaltenders in Ken Dryden and a powerful offense led by Guy Lafleur. Beating the Canadiens was never easy for the Bruins, and it wasn't about to get easier for the 1979 playoffs. Going into game six of the series, the Canadiens needed just one more win to move onto the Stanley Cup final. It was desperation time for the Bruins, and they knew it. They were relying on the scoring talent of Jean Ratelle and the goaltending of legend Gerry Cheevers. But it was Jonathan who became the hero of the game when he scored a hat trick to help the Bruins beat the Canadiens by a score of 5–2, sending the series into a seventh and deciding game.

With a renewed sense of purpose, the Bruins walked into the Montreal Forum ready to dispense with the Canadiens. The Bruins seemed to have it all wrapped up in the dying minutes of the third period, nervously holding onto a 3–2 lead. But then disaster struck.

These are Jonathan's own words on what occurred next, taken from the book by Don Marks, *They Call Me Chief*:

> "Our strategy all game had been to put Don Marcotte on Guy Lafleur. Lafleur headed to the Montreal bench and it was our line's turn to go on. Wayne Cashman and I looked over for a signal but Grapes (Cherry) wasn't even watching the game! He was arguing with some fans who were harassing him from behind the bench. So we jumped on the ice. Anyways, when Cherry turned back to face the play, he sent Rick Middleton out and the game went on. That's how far the play had gone on...but I never really knew what was happening until the whistle blew and they called us for too many men on the ice."

With the man advantage, Guy Lafleur broke into the Boston zone and blasted the tying goal past Bruins goaltender Gilles Gilbert. In overtime, Yvon Lambert of the Habs took a cross-ice pass from Mario Tremblay and scored the series' winner. The Canadiens had burned the Bruins again. That series was Jonathan's last real shot at the Stanley Cup, and the memory of it burns him to this day.

The 1979–80 season was a rebound year for Jonathan; he scored 21 points and 14 assists and racked up 208 penalty minutes. All those minutes spent in the box were a result of his physical play and his take-no-grief attitude, but all the grinding in the corners and the punches to the face took their toll on his body. As any retired NHL "tough guy" would attest, their careers are long on excitement but short on length; many are forced into early retirement because of injury. Only a few lucky ones are able to have long careers.

Jonathan wasn't one of the lucky ones. As the injuries mounted and his physical presence on the ice began to diminish, the Bruins lost interest in his services. It also didn't help that Jonathan's number-one fan Don Cherry had been fired by management after the playoff loss to the Canadiens and that the new coach Fred Creighton wanted to take the Bruins in a different direction. As Jonathan's injuries began to mount, his shifts began to shrink to the point where he wasn't of any use to Boston. In 1983 he was traded to the Pittsburgh Penguins for cash, and he lasted only 19 games in Pittsburgh before hanging up his skates for good.

After retirement Jonathan moved back to his community where he continued to play hockey for fun in local senior leagues. Just into his 30s, he was far from senior, but getting back to playing the game for fun and being close to his family was a full-circle moment for Jonathan. He continues to live on the "rez," plays hockey when he can and gives back to the community through his charity work.

Stats

Season	Team	Games Played	Goals	Assists	Points	Penalties
1975–76	Boston Bruins	1	0	0	0	0
1976–77	Boston Bruins	69	17	13	30	69
1977–78	Boston Bruins	68	27	25	52	116
1978–79	Boston Bruins	33	6	9	15	96
1979–80	Boston Bruins	79	21	19	40	208
1980–81	Boston Bruins	74	14	24	38	192
1981–82	Boston Bruins	67	6	17	23	57
1982–83	Boston Bruins	1	0	0	0	0
	Pittsburgh Penguins	19	0	3	3	13
NHL Totals		411	91	110	201	751

Blair
Atcheynum

OF CREE DESCENT, BLAIR ATCHEYNUM was born on April 20, 1969, in Estevan, Saskatchewan.

He got his start in professional hockey with the Western Hockey League's Saskatoon Blades, before moving on to the Moose Jaw Warriors where he began to blossom as a player.

In the 1987–88 season he scored 32 goals in 60 games, but by the next season he had more than doubled that mark with 70 goals in 71 games. With numbers like that, Blair didn't have to wait long at the 1989 NHL Entry Draft. Surprisingly, after the first two rounds, no team had yet selected the big 6-foot-2, 210-pound right wing, but then the Hartford Whalers came calling and selected him 52nd overall.

For the next three years Atcheynum languished in the minors waiting for his moment with the Whalers. It never came. He never seemed to figure into the Whalers' plans, and in 1992, the Ottawa Senators claimed him in the Expansion Draft.

With the Senators he got to play in his first four NHL games, but the rest of the season was spent in the minors. Over the next four years, the NHL tested Atcheynum's patience even further after he bounced around to several different teams before finally getting another shot with the big leagues, this time with the St. Louis Blues.

He played in 61 games with the Blues and scored 11 goals and 15 assists. But the Blues were not overly impressed and shipped him to Nashville for a season before again acquiring him through a trade. Atcheynum played 12 games with the Blues before he was again traded, this time to the Chicago Blackhawks. In Chicago he played 47 games during the 1999–2000 season and scored five goals. He jumped back and forth from the Hawks to the minors over the next two seasons before finally playing his last game in the NHL in 2001.

Although Atcheynum achieved the dream of making it into the NHL, he was never able to catch a break and land a solid job, but he never regretted it one bit.

Stats

Season	Team	Games Played	Goals	Assists	Points	Penalties
1992–93	Ottawa Senators	4	0	1	1	0
1997–98	St. Louis Blues	61	11	15	26	10
1998–99	Nashville Predators	53	8	6	14	16
1999–2000	St. Louis Blues	12	2	2	4	2
	Chicago Blackhawks	47	5	7	12	6
2000–01	Chicago Blackhawks	19	1	2	3	2
NHL Totals		196	27	33	60	36

George Armstrong

GEORGE ARMSTRONG WAS THE FIRST Native hockey player to achieve lasting success in the NHL, and also the first to have his name engraved on hockey's most hallowed of shrines, the Stanley Cup.

Born in Skead, Ontario, in 1930 to a father of Irish descent and an Algonquin mother, George grew up without much knowledge of his culture. Since the family lived off the reserve, George did what any other kid his age in the small towns of Ontario did; he played hockey.

His hockey skills developed quickly, and so did his size. By the age of 16 he was already much bigger than some of his friends. His size made him awkward, but on the ice it gave him an advantage. By the time he was 16 years old he was already the star on the Copper Cliff Redmen of the Northern Ontario

Hockey Association, playing alongside future team-mate Tim Horton.

The two players caught the attention of the Toronto Maple Leafs and were soon brought in under their umbrella. Armstrong signed a negotiating contract with the Leafs and moved south to Stratford where he starred with the Kroehlers. Although he was never a pure scoring forward, he was a master of the game in all aspects of his position. Defensively, he was a challenge to play against, and on the offense he could always surprise. Armstrong never scored more than 23 goals in one season throughout his NHL career, but he was always the consistent player whom coaches could rely on.

Playing with the poise and skill of a much older player, Armstrong could not be kept down in the minors for long, and the Maple Leafs called him up to action for his first taste of the NHL in the middle of the 1949–50 season. He was called back up to the Leafs two years later for the 1951–52 season and remained with the Leafs for the rest of his playing days.

After Armstrong's first season, Maple Leafs and general hockey legend King Clancy was captivated by Armstrong style of play and was not shy to lay on the compliments to the rookie.

"This kid's got everything. He has size, speed, and he can shoot 'em into the net better than any hockey player I've known in a long time. I'll be surprised if he doesn't become a superstar," said Clancy.

His words could not have been any truer. From 1951 to 1971, Armstrong played in 1185 games as a member of the Toronto Maple Leafs. When he joined the Leafs they had just come off some of the most successful seasons in the franchise's history in the late '40s and early '50s. But soon after Armstrong joined the Leafs, the NHL saw the rise of the Montreal Canadiens and the Detroit Red Wings as the league powerhouse teams, and getting into the playoffs proved difficult. But Armstrong always showed up game after game and gave the same consistent effort. Not a lot of goals were scored back then, but Armstrong scored an average of 15 to 20 goals per season, and that was worth a lot in the NHL. He became such a fixture on the team that when captain Ted Kennedy retired after the 1956–57 season, Armstrong was handed the leadership of the team.

With the dawn of the 1960s and the addition of some new blood to the team, the Leafs began to turn their fortunes around and finally saw some positive changes.

During the 1961–62 season, Armstrong had his best season in terms of points production, scoring 21 goals and 32 assists. But it was in the playoffs that the new captain showed what he was truly made of, scoring seven goals and leading the Leafs to their first Stanley Cup in 11 years. It was also the first time a Native hockey player had won the Cup, and he also happened to be the captain.

That Cup was the first of three consecutive Stanley Cups the Leafs won. Nearly a decade into his career, Armstrong was still in his prime and led his team to the championships. By 1967, the Leafs' core group of players, such as Armstrong, Allan Stanley, Tim Horton, Bob Baun and Johnny Bower, were getting up there in age, and no one expected that a bunch of old guys could compete against the likes of the Montreal Canadiens, a team full of young talent who had won the two previous Stanley Cups. But somehow Armstrong was able to lead his boys through and win the last Stanley Cup ever given to the Toronto Maple Leafs thus far.

When the league expanded and the season got longer, Armstrong felt the call of retirement. In 1971 he decided to hang up his skates for good. He coached for several years with the Toronto Marlboros and had a brief return to Maple Leaf Gardens when he got behind the Maple Leafs bench halfway through the 1988–89 season. After his time behind the bench that year, he left the game for good to enjoy his retirement.

George Armstrong is a member of the Hockey Hall of Fame and is a proud reminder to his people of what can be accomplished.

Stats

Season	Team	Games Played	Goals	Assists	Points	Penalties
1949–50	Toronto Maple Leafs	2	0	0	0	0
1951–52	Toronto Maple Leafs	20	3	3	6	30
1952–53	Toronto Maple Leafs	52	14	11	25	54
1953–54	Toronto Maple Leafs	63	17	15	32	60
1954–55	Toronto Maple Leafs	66	10	18	28	80
1955–56	Toronto Maple Leafs	67	16	32	48	97
1956–57	Toronto Maple Leafs	54	18	26	44	37
1957–58	Toronto Maple Leafs	59	17	25	42	93
1958–59	Toronto Maple Leafs	59	20	16	36	37
1959–60	Toronto Maple Leafs	70	23	28	51	60
1960–61	Toronto Maple Leafs	47	14	19	33	21
1961–62	Toronto Maple Leafs	70	21	32	53	27
1962–63	Toronto Maple Leafs	70	19	24	43	27
1963–64	Toronto Maple Leafs	66	20	17	37	14
1964–65	Toronto Maple Leafs	59	15	22	34	14
1965–66	Toronto Maple Leafs	70	16	35	51	12
1966–67	Toronto Maple Leafs	70	9	24	33	26
1967–68	Toronto Maple Leafs	62	13	21	34	4
1968–69	Toronto Maple Leafs	53	11	16	27	10
1969–70	Toronto Maple Leafs	49	13	15	28	12
1970–71	Toronto Maple Leafs	59	7	18	25	6
NHL Totals		1187	296	417	713	721

Henry
Boucha

BORN ON JUNE 1, 1951, just outside Warroad, Minnesota, to his Chippewa mother and Ojibway, Cree and French father, Henry Charles Boucha was drawn to hockey at an early age. By the time he was in the sixth grade, Henry had helped his bantam hockey team win the Minnesota state championship.

The large defenseman's star continued to rise in high school when he was voted to the Minnesota All-State team three years in a row. But it was during his senior year that Boucha made a name for himself in the hockey world and began to catch the attention of NHL scouts.

The Warroad hockey team was by far the underdog of the year-end tournaments, but Boucha made them a better team and was instrumental in getting the squad all the way into the final against a team from Edina, Minnesota. Edina is a wealthy neighborhood just outside Minneapolis, with a large school and a greater pool of talented players to choose from, but Boucha and his bunch from Warroad were not about to be intimidated by some rich kids. Edina did manage to win the game, but only by a 5–4 margin in overtime. The Warroad team showed true grit, and Boucha put up a formidable wall along his blue line and made Edina pay the price every time they wanted in the zone. Despite the loss, scouts and agents soon came knocking on Boucha's door.

The University of Minnesota came calling as well, offering him a full scholarship to attend their school and play for their hockey team, but Boucha instead chose to play junior hockey in Winnipeg. It was in the Canadian Hockey League that Boucha was switched from defense to forward. The coach realized that with Boucha's excellent skating ability and large frame, he could make an imposing power forward. The switch was a success, and in 1970 his talent was recognized enough to get a call to play for the U.S. National Hockey team. Boucha was also selected 16th overall in the 1971 NHL Amateur Draft by the Detroit Red Wings. But before he could make his debut in the NHL, the U.S. National team invited him to participate in the 1972 Olympics.

Henry Boucha and his National teammates were sent over to Japan to battle a skilled group of international opponents. The United States was not expected to go far in the tournament with hockey powerhouses like the Soviet Union, Finland and Sweden all vying for medals. The Americans surprised everyone by making it into the final against the high-powered Soviet squad. Unfortunately for Boucha, he had to settle for a silver medal, but it was as good as gold for the kid from Warroad, Minnesota. In the six games he played in, Boucha was among the top 10 in scoring, netting two goals and four assists.

Immediately after his stellar Olympic performance, he was called into action by the Detroit Red Wings and given his first chance at making the roster. Cracking the lineup, however, proved to be a difficult task, and as often happens with young rookie sensations, Boucha was sent back down to the minors. The 16 games he played in the 1971–72 season were not a complete loss, though, as he was able to get the first goal of his NHL career out of the way. The next year he returned and earned a full-time spot in the Wings' lineup.

Boucha made an immediate connection with the fans and media as he was never afraid to express his opinions and was instantly recognizable on the ice with his long hair and white headband.

As happens with most hockey players, once you have established your position on the team, it is common to be given a nickname; Boucha's was "Chief." Several Native groups complained of the "offensive" moniker, but Boucha never complained once.

After two full seasons, despite putting up respectable numbers, Boucha was traded to the Minnesota North Stars for forward Danny Grant. Despite Boucha's numbers and popularity on the team, management could not pass up the deal for Grant, considering that he had consistently scored 20–30 goals per season. For Boucha, the trade was a good opportunity to make a name for himself on a young team and play in his home state. But just halfway through the season, Boucha suffered a terrifying injury.

On January 4, 1975, in a game against the Boston Bruins, Boucha and the Bruins Dave Forbes got into a fight, and in the ensuing scrum Forbes deliberately smashed the butt-end of his stick in Boucha's eye. The assault broke Boucha's eye socket, and the gash it left required 30 stitches to close.

After the game, the local Minnesota district attorney filed assault charges against Forbes for his attack on Boucha. As it was the first time that charges had ever been laid by civil authorities for an incident that occurred in a professional sport, the jury was split down the middle, and the trial ended without a result. Boucha for his part was unsatisfied with the outcome of the trial and ended up suing Dave Forbes, the Bruins and the NHL for the injuries he sustained. The lawsuit ended in a settlement for Boucha that was rumored to be in the $1.5 million range.

The season after the eye injury, Boucha was traded to the Kansas City Scouts where he played just 28 games, and then the following season he was traded to the Colorado Rockies where he played only nine games. His loss of ice time was directly related to the injury suffered in the fight with Forbes, which gave him constant headaches and fits of double vision. At the young age of 26, Boucha was forced into retirement.

But despite having his career cut short, he still made an impact on the sport. In 1995, he became the first person of Native American heritage to be inducted into the United States Hockey Hall of Fame for his contributions at the professional level and for helping the U.S. National team exceed expectations at the 1972 Winter Olympics.

Stats

Season	Team	Games Played	Goals	Assists	Points	Penalties
1971–72	Detroit Red Wings	16	1	0	1	2
1972–73	Detroit Red Wings	73	14	14	28	82
1973–74	Detroit Red Wings	70	19	12	31	32
1974–75	Minnesota North Stars	51	15	14	29	23
1975–76	Kansas City Scouts	28	4	7	11	14
1976–77	Colorado Rockies	9	0	2	2	4
NHL Totals		247	53	49	102	157

Gary
Sargent

AN ANISHINAABE NATIVE from the Red Lake Indian
Reservation in northern Minnesota, Gary Sargent
had plenty of ice to practice his hockey skills on
as a child. The deep cold winters offered the perfect
training ground for the NHLer in the making.
At five years of age, the young Sargent was
already out on the ice in the dead of winter with
the other boys on the reserve. With an obvious
dedication to the sport at such an early age, Sargent's
parents happily enrolled the energetic youngster
in the local hockey league, and his talents quickly
developed.

But hockey was not his only passion, and when
the ice was gone, during the summer Sargent was
an avid baseball and football player. His baseball
prowess reached such a level during high school

that upon graduation he had offers to try out for the Minnesota Twins as well as several football scholarships, but he turned them all down and chose the hockey route instead. He enrolled at Bemidji State College in 1972 and quickly became one of the best players on the school's team. In his freshman season the star defenseman was named to the All-Star team and was voted as the league's Most Valuable Player. In 1974, Sargent's abilities on the ice were at such a level that he was invited by the U.S. National Hockey Team to join the junior squad on a trip to the Soviet Union to play in the first unofficial Junior World Championships. It was at this tournament that he caught the eye of several NHL scouts.

The Los Angeles Kings were so impressed with the kid from Minnesota that they drafted Sargent as their first choice overall. After spending one year with the Kings' minor league affiliate, he finally got the call he had been waiting for, which came just in time for the start of the 1975–76 season. Seizing the opportunity, Sargent had an excellent rookie season and earned the honor of being named the Kings' top rookie. The offensive defenseman was exactly what the Kings had needed on defense. Stuck in a division with the powerful Montreal Canadiens, Sargent's first year in the NHL provided him with a major learning curve, and in the following year he only got better.

Playing with the likes of Marcel Dionne and Butch Goring, Sargent finished the 1976–77 season as the Kings' top-scoring defenseman. That year was also Sargent's first taste of playoff hockey, and the added pressure did not bother him on the ice. He helped the Kings power past the Atlanta Flames in the preliminary round and put in a valiant fight against the Boston Bruins but ended up losing the series in six games.

Sargent had another good season in 1977–78 and again led the team's defense in scoring, with 41 points. But after an early playoff exit at the hands of the Toronto Maple Leafs in the preliminary round, Sargent ended his tenure with the Kings and moved back to his home state to play with the Minnesota North Stars.

Although Sargent enjoyed being back home, the North Stars were one of the league's bottom-feeding teams. After one full season with the Stars in which he performed up to his usual standard, Sargent was plagued with injuries. Over the next three seasons he consistently missed games because of a back problem and was kept out for long stretches to undergo multiple surgeries.

He went from playing 79 games in his first season with the North Stars to just 15 games by the end of the 1981–82 season. Despite the nagging pain in his back, Sargent still wanted to play and came back the following season. But luck did not go his way, and he was forced out at the end of the season when he suffered a debilitating knee injury that required him to retire.

After briefly working as a scout for the Los Angeles Kings, Sargent returned to his community, took a job as a conservation officer and continued his involvement with the game by coaching the local youth teams on the reserve.

Stats

Season	Team	Games Played	Goals	Assists	Points	Penalties
1975–76	Los Angeles Kings	63	8	16	24	36
1976–77	Los Angeles Kings	80	14	40	54	65
1977–78	Los Angeles Kings	72	7	34	41	52
1978–79	Minnesota North Stars	79	12	32	44	39
1979–80	Minnesota North Stars	52	13	21	34	22
1980–81	Minnesota North Stars	23	4	7	11	36
1981–82	Minnesota North Stars	15	0	5	5	18
1982–83	Minnesota North Stars	18	3	6	9	5
NHL Totals		402	61	161	222	273

John
Chabot

BORN IN SUMMERSIDE, Prince Edward Island, in May 1962, John Chabot and his family, who were of Algonquin decent, moved to Hull, Quebec, early in his life. A gifted hockey player in high school, the crafty center was drafted into the Quebec Major Junior Hockey League (QMJHL) first overall by the Hull Olympiques in 1978.

Chabot fit in perfectly with the Olympiques, and after two good seasons he caught the attention of the Montreal Canadiens, who used their third pick, 40th overall, to select him at the 1980 NHL Entry Draft. After a few more years languishing in the minors, Chabot received the call to play with the Montreal Canadiens for the start of the 1983–84 season.

He had finally realized a dream of playing in the NHL, and the rookie made a good impression in his first year, playing in 56 games and scoring a respectable 18 goals and 25 assists. His tenure with the Canadiens was brief, however, as the Habs wanted a more seasoned center and traded him 10 games into the 1984–85 season for Pittsburgh Penguins center Ron Flockhart.

Making the transition from a good team at the time to one of the worst in the league wasn't easy for the young Chabot, but playing on the same team as a young Mario Lemieux wasn't all that bad.

Chabot stayed with the Penguins up until the 1986–87 season and scored an average of 14 goals per season. Looking to explore the free-agent market during the off-season, he was scooped up by the Detroit Red Wings. In his first year with the team he had his best points season, racking up 13 goals and 44 assists for 57 points. He was also instrumental to the Red Wings' push in the playoffs that saw them get all the way to the Conference finals before getting knocked out by the powerhouse Edmonton Oilers.

Chabot's next season was cut short by injury, and as his fortunes waned, so did that of the Red Wings. After two more seasons with the Wings, Chabot decided that playing 27 games a season and scoring only five goals was indication enough that he should retire from the game. At the end of the 1990–91 season, he hung up his skates for good.

But Chabot didn't stay out of hockey completely. He entered the new and always frustrating world of coaching in the QMJHL. He honed his leadership skills as coach for his old team, the Olympique de Hull/Gatineau, and then went over to the Acadie-Bathurst Titans before making the jump back into the high-pressure stakes of the NHL as an assistant coach for the New York Islanders.

Stats

Season	Team	Games Played	Goals	Assists	Points	Penalties
1983–84	Montreal Canadiens	56	18	25	43	13
1984–85	Montreal Canadiens	10	1	6	7	2
	Pittsburgh Penguins	67	8	45	53	12
1985–86	Pittsburgh Penguins	77	14	31	45	6
1986–87	Pittsburgh Penguins	72	14	22	36	8
1987–88	Detroit Red Wings	78	13	44	57	10
1988–89	Detroit Red Wings	52	2	10	12	6
1989–90	Detroit Red Wings	69	9	40	49	24
1990–91	Detroit Red Wings	27	5	5	10	4
NHL Totals		508	84	228	312	85

Kimbi
Daniels

LIKE MANY BEFORE HIM, Estevan, Saskatchewan
native Kimbi Daniels had always dreamed of making it to the NHL, but he also realized that few ever
did. However, odds were never an issue that kept
Daniels from pursuing his dreams.

Leaving Estevan, Daniels started his career with
the Swift Current Broncos of the Western Hockey
League. It was with Swift Current that he caught
the eye of Philadelphia Flyers scouts who used
their fifth choice, 44th overall, to select him in the
1990 Entry Draft.

While the trend had been for the Flyers to select
the largest rookies, Daniels, at 5 feet 10 inches,
175 pounds, was not their typical selection. But the
"diminutive" center had more than enough heart
to make it to the NHL.

In his first season in 1990–91, however, the Flyers only gave him two games in which to prove himself before sending him back down to their minor league affiliate. It wasn't until the 1991–92 season that the Flyers decided to give him a chance at cracking the lineup.

Daniels got a fair chance at making it in the NHL, and in 25 games he scored only one goal and one assist. Everything seemed to be going fine, but then he suffered a knee and leg injury that forced him out of the lineup for the rest of the season. It also proved to be an injury that pushed him out of the NHL for good.

But hockey was in his blood, and Daniels wasn't going to stop playing just because he couldn't break back into the NHL. He spent the next several years bouncing around different leagues, and he now makes his living in the East Coast Hockey League with the Phoenix Roadrunners.

Stats

Season	Team	Games Played	Goals	Assists	Points	Penalties
1990–91	Philadelphia Flyers	2	0	1	1	0
1991–92	Philadelphia Flyers	25	1	1	2	4
NHL Totals		27	1	2	3	4

Scott
Daniels

Born and raised on the Cree Mistawasis First Nation Reserve in north central Saskatchewan, Daniels did not have the same opportunities as other kids in Canada, but there was always hockey, and he fully embraced the sport.

Moving up through the community hockey ranks, Daniels began to make a name for himself as a sprightly forward with a penchant for the physical side of the game. Playing this style of "tough guy" hockey got him noticed, and at 17 he began his path to the NHL when he signed with the Kamloops Blazers of the Western Hockey League (WHL). Bouncing around a few teams in the WHL from 1986 to 1989, Daniels became a player known for dropping the gloves on occasion but also as a forward who could drive to the net and contribute with a few goals. The energy he brought to the game and his imposing 6-foot-3, 215-pound frame caught the attention of several NHL teams, but it was the Hartford Whalers that landed him 136th overall at the 1989 Entry Draft.

Despite the positive turn of events, it took Daniels another three years before he made it to the big leagues. During those three years from 1990 to 1993, he played with the Springfield Indians of the American Hockey League (AHL) and was a major reason the Indians won two consecutive Calder Cup Trophies in 1990 and 1991. His dominating presence on the ice and his ability to go to the net were a major reason for his success, and finally in 1993 the Hartford Whalers called him up for his first NHL game against the Boston Bruins.

Wanting to show that he could play with the big boys, that night Daniels hit anything and everything on the ice with a Bruins jersey. He also wasn't shy to drop the gloves, and by the end of his first NHL game he had 19 minutes in penalties. But as quickly as he had made it to the NHL, Daniels was sent back down. After playing another season in the AHL, he was called back up by the Whalers but only played a total of 12 games. However, by the 1995–96 season, he had firmly established himself with the Whalers and found himself playing 53 games that year. The enforcer role was not something he relished, but Daniels did not mind performing if it kept him playing in the best league in the world. Placed alongside Kelly Chase and Mark Janssens, the trio became known as the "Destruction Line," regularly put in the game to physically intimidate the opposing team and police for their best players.

One of Daniels' most memorable moments of on-ice intimidation came during a 1996 game when the Whalers played host to the Buffalo Sabres. At one point in the game, Sabres' enforcer Rob Ray went after Whalers captain Brendan Shanahan near the Hartford bench. Daniels, who was not on the ice at the time, witnessed the confrontation and decided to jump off the bench and attack Ray directly. Somehow Daniels ended up on Buffalo's bench, and upon losing hold of Ray, he simply grabbed for any blue Buffalo jersey nearby. It took several minutes for the referee and linesman to extricate Daniels from the Buffalo bench and to restore order to the game.

On top of his 254 minutes in penalties that year, Daniels scored three goals and recorded four assists. It was a big difference from his days in the minor leagues, but Daniels savored every moment he could.

During the off-season, Daniels decided to test the free-agent market and was signed by the Philadelphia Flyers, who were always in search of an imposing roster. Daniels fit in well with the likes of Dan Kordic, Eric Lindros and Daniel Lacroix. In 56 games, the 26-year-old left-winger scored five goals, three assists and racked up a team-leading 237 penalty minutes.

However, with several fighters already on the team, the Flyers wanted to take a new course and did not see Daniels in their future. During the 1997 off-season he was placed on waivers and picked up by the New Jersey Devils. His tenure with the Devils didn't last long as he only played 26 games during the 1997–98 season and one game in 1998–99. Unable to find steady work in the NHL, Daniels retired from pro hockey.

Stats

Season	Team	Games Played	Goals	Assists	Points	Penalties
1992–93	Hartford Whalers	1	0	0	0	19
1994–95	Hartford Whalers	12	0	2	2	55
1995–96	Hartford Whalers	53	3	4	7	254
1996–97	Philadelphia Flyers	56	5	3	8	237
1997–98	New Jersey Devils	26	0	3	3	102
1998–99	New Jersey Devils	1	0	0	0	0
NHL Totals		149	8	12	20	667

Ron
Delorme

RON DELORME HAS BEEN AROUND hockey for nearly his entire life—from the first time he put on a pair of skates growing up as a kid in North Battleford, Saskatchewan, to his current job as chief of amateur scouting for the Vancouver Canucks.

As is the story with most professional hockey players, Delorme's love affair with the game began from an early age. Being from North Battleford, there was not much else for a young boy to do in the winter but play hockey, and Delorme soon found that he had a talent to offer.

But he almost quit playing hockey, not because of the cost or that he could not match the talent of the other kids, but because the racial taunting was becoming too much for him. "I started getting known as this 'wagonburner.' I really had a rough time to deal with it," said Delorme looking back. But he stuck it out, and his tenacity paid off.

Delorme began his professional hockey career at the age of 18 with the Swift Current Broncos of the Western Canada Hockey League (WCHL) in 1973. He was the kind of player every coach loves to have on a team. The highly energetic center was not always the top scorer on the team, but he could be relied upon to work hard every shift. His feet were constantly in motion, and if he didn't have the puck, he was chasing the guy who did. After two seasons in the WCHL, Delorme had the privilege of being scouted by NHL teams and scouts from the new start-up pro-league, the World Hockey Association (WHA). The Kansas City Scouts of the NHL drafted him 56th overall in the 1975 Amateur Draft, and the Denver Spurs of the WHA claimed ownership of him as well. The NHL seemed the farthest away, so when the Denver Spurs offered him a rookie contract, Delorme jumped at the chance to play pro hockey alongside NHL cast-offs such as former Montreal Canadiens Ralph Backstrom. But Delorme's honeymoon in the pros did not last long, and after 22 games and one goal, he was sent back down to the minors.

Just one year later, the Colorado Rockies (originally the Kansas City Scouts) came calling, pulled Delorme out of the minors and stuck him into the lineup for the start of the 1976–77 season. Although the Rockies were not the best team in the NHL (they were in fact the second worst), they gave Delorme the opportunity to play regular games and shifts, something that never would have happened had he tried to crack the Montreal Canadiens lineup at the time.

By his freshman season, Delorme had established himself in the league as an energetic forward, skilled on the forecheck and a special teams' player. The local papers even called him the hardest working winger in the NHL.

But it wasn't just Delorme's hard work that had made an impression on players and coaches around the league. Although he never fit the definition of the classic enforcer, when called upon, he could scrap with the best and toughest of the NHL. In one game in particular, Delorme caught the eye of a man known for loving tough, physical hockey. During a game between the Rockies and head coach Don Cherry's Boston Bruins, Delorme did something the Cherry had never seen in an NHL game. "We had a real tough team in Boston, with plenty of punching power in the lineup," said Cherry in the book *They Call Me Chief.*

"Well, I never saw anything like what I saw the first time we played against Delorme. First period, this skinny Indian kid fights

Terry O'Reilly to a standstill. Second period, he takes John Wensink on and holds his own. Finally, in the third period, he goes at it with Stan Jonathan. One guy, and he takes on our toughest guys, one by one, period by period. Ron Delorme was a good clean fighter. No dirty stuff. Just straight up, blow for blow, and he wouldn't back down from any of them. Fighting takes a lot out of a player. To be able to keep going like that in the third period was incredible. I think Ronnie is the only guy who has ever done that."

After the last fight with Stan Jonathan, a Native himself, Stan said to Delorme as the linesmen were breaking them up, "You know, Ron, Natives shouldn't be fighting Natives." Both of the players agreed that night that brothers should not be fighting brothers, and that there were plenty of other players who they could take on in the league.

After five good years with the Rockies, Delorme was put on waivers when the Rockies franchise folded. The Vancouver Canucks quickly snapped him up.

In his first season with the Canucks, Delorme's goal production was down from previous years, but he was proving to be a reliable forechecker and was able to change the pace of a game with his physical play. He nearly tripled his time in the penalty box during his first year with the Canucks, from 70 minutes in 1980–81 to 177 minutes in 1981–82. It was that first year with the Canucks that Delorme got his first real taste of the NHL playoffs when the Canucks went all the way to the Stanley Cup finals against the New York Islanders. He played in 15 of the Canucks' 18 games and was instrumental in knocking off the Los Angeles Kings and the Chicago Blackhawks. But all the energy and spunk in the world could not keep the Canucks from falling to the more talented and powerful Islanders, who swept the series on their way to their third of four straight Stanley Cups.

With each successive season, Delorme played fewer and fewer games. He just didn't seem to have the energy that he once had, and the Canucks were giving his ice time to the younger guys. A knee injury in 1985 gave Delorme the final reason he needed to hang up his skates and say goodbye to playing pro hockey. But his life in hockey was still in its infancy.

During his time as a player in Vancouver, Delorme not only became part of the team, but he also became a member of the Canuck family, and over the next 15 years after his retirement he acted mainly as one of the club's scouts before being promoted to chief of amateur scouting in 2000.

Recognizing how far he had come in life, Delorme wanted to give young Native kids the chance at having a career like he had in hockey; he opened up the Aboriginal Role Models Hockey School in the late 1990s in Saskatoon. This was his way of responding to the odd lack of Aboriginal players who make it into the professional ranks. The school provides young players a place to hone their skills and show them off to scouts when they otherwise would languish in obscurity.

Throughout his career Delorme has never backed away from his heritage and has always made his people proud by giving back to the community that had given him so much.

Stats

Season	Team	Games Played	Goals	Assists	Points	Penalties
1976–77	Colorado Rockies	29	6	4	10	23
1977–78	Colorado Rockies	68	10	11	21	47
1978–79	Colorado Rockies	77	20	8	28	68
1979–80	Colorado Rockies	75	19	24	43	76
1980–81	Colorado Rockies	65	11	16	27	70
1981–82	Vancouver Canucks	59	9	8	17	177
1982–83	Vancouver Canucks	56	5	8	13	87
1983–84	Vancouver Canucks	64	2	2	4	68
1984–85	Vancouver Canucks	31	1	2	3	51
NHL Totals		524	83	83	166	667

Dan Frawley

FOR A PLAYER WHO WAS DRAFTED 204th overall in the 1980 NHL Entry Draft, Dan Frawley managed to stay in the professional ranks a long time compared with some of the other young players drafted so late.

Born in 1962, in Sturgeon Falls, Ontario, Frawley made a name for himself in the hockey world like many Native players before him, not with his skills with the puck but by the power of his punches. Despite his predilection for getting into scraps, Frawley was a valuable team member, always willing to work hard and never one to enter into a fight without cause.

His path to the NHL started with the Sudbury Wolves of the Ontario Hockey Association and then with the Cornwall Royals of the Quebec Major Junior Hockey League. In his first season with the

Wolves, Frawley's role was less as a fighter and more of the goal scorer, potting 21 goals in 63 games with just 67 minutes in penalties. But as his career in the juniors progressed, his goal output remained the same while his time spent in the sin bin increased exponentially. By his third season in the junior ranks he had tallied 27 goals but increased his penalty time to 239 minutes.

His ability to play a physical game and score goals made him a rare commodity among young hockey players. It was these qualities that the Chicago Blackhawks were looking for when they drafted him 204th overall in the 1980 Entry Draft.

After spending two more years with the Hawks' American Hockey League affiliate the Springfield Indians, Frawley put up impressive numbers, scoring 30 goals and 27 assists in the 1982–83 season, and he continued that pace with 22 goals and 34 assists in 69 games the following season. With those numbers, the Hawks felt confident enough to bring the young Frawley up for his first taste of NHL action. His stay was brief. Playing in only three games and not recording a single statistic, Frawley was sent back down to the minors. The next season, he was called to action mid-way through the Blackhawks' 1984–85 campaign and got the time he needed to make a significant impression on the league. He played in 30 games, scored four goals and three assists and tallied 64 minutes in penalties. He was also given his first taste of NHL playoff action, but it was only a few shifts in one game.

During the off-season, the Blackhawks did not see Frawley fitting in with their future plans and placed him on waivers. The Pittsburgh Penguins saw potential in the young right winger and added him to their lineup for the start of the 1985–86 season. The Penguins proved to be the perfect fit for Frawley. On top of his role as one of the team's tough guys, he was given the freedom to explore a deeper role with the team. During his first two years in Pittsburgh he wasn't one of the most prolific scorers, but he had become one of the team's leaders on and off the ice. He was so important to the unity of the team that he was named its captain in October 1987.

Frawley's tenure as captain did not last long, as just two short months later he suffered an injury that took him out of the lineup for an extended period. The captaincy of the Penguins was handed over to Mario Lemieux, and Frawley never got it back.

Frawley's injury continued into the 1988–89 season, playing healthy for just 46 games. It proved to be his final season in the NHL as he was sent down to the minors and never made a return.

Stats

Season	Team	Games Played	Goals	Assists	Points	Penalties
1983–84	Chicago Blackhawks	3	0	0	0	0
1984–85	Chicago Blackhawks	30	4	3	7	64
1985–86	Pittsburgh Penguins	69	10	11	21	174
1986–87	Pittsburgh Penguins	78	14	14	28	218
1987–88	Pittsburgh Penguins	47	6	8	14	152
1988–89	Pittsburgh Penguins	46	3	4	7	66
NHL Totals		273	37	40	77	674

Ted
Hodgson

ALTHOUGH TED HODGSON, a Cree from Hobbema, Alberta, got to live his dream of playing in the NHL, it was unfortunately for only four games during the 1966–67 season with the Boston Bruins.

Just one year before the league expanded from six to 12 teams, Hodgson did not have much of a chance to crack the NHL with the amount of talent that was already in place.

Unable to break into the NHL, Hodgson spent the remainder of his career bouncing around semi-pro leagues and played a few years in the fledgling World Hockey Association before retiring in 1977.

Stats

Season	Team	Games Played	Goals	Assists	Points	Penalties
1966–67	Boston Bruins	4	0	0	0	6
NHL Totals		4	0	0	0	6

Wayne
King

BORN OF OJIBWAY ANCESTRY, Wayne King's story is like that of many young Native hockey players aspiring to make it to the NHL. Years of their lives are given to this pursuit, and few are lucky enough to get their skates on a professional arena let alone have a full NHL career. King's path to the NHL puts him about in the middle of the two—he got to taste the fruits of his labors but not long enough to call it a career.

Wayne was born in the tiny Ontario town of Fort McNicoll in 1951, and the Kings were the only Native family in town. Having not much else to occupy his time during the long winters, Wayne took up hockey. He showed a clear talent for the game, and by the time he was in his teenage years he was invited to try out for the Niagara Falls Flyers of the Ontario Hockey League. He didn't make the team the first time around, but on his second attempt he was signed to his first minor league contract, and the entire family packed up and moved to Niagara Falls.

For the next three years, King worked hard on his game, and though he was not a natural goal scorer, he proved to have a unique talent as a defensive forward. But getting into the NHL at the start of the 1970s was not an easy proposition. Despite the league's expansion a few years earlier, jobs were still at a premium. But luckily for King, a new team had joined the league in 1970, and they were looking for some young talent to fill out their lineup.

King was signed to the California Golden Seals' farm team in 1971, and two years later he was finally called up to play in his first NHL game for the 1973–74 season. He only played two games and was sent back down to the minors. For the 1974–75 season he hoped to turn things around and prove that he deserved a place in the NHL, but the hockey gods were not on his side. After playing in a few games, he was sidelined with a knee injury and then shortly after returning to action was taken out again, but this time because of a burst appendix. He played 25 games that season, scoring four goals and seven assists. It wasn't exactly the debut he had planned, but the Seals had committed to keeping him for another season, and King hoped to turn things around for the better.

The 1975–76 season was one of promise for King, but it turned out to be one of failed hopes and missed opportunities. He played 46 games during that season and never was able to display the confidence and skill that was his trademark in the minor leagues. He wanted another chance at redemption, but at the end of the season the California Golden Seals folded operations, and King was left without a job. He played a few more years in the minors, and when no NHL clubs seemed to be showing any interest, he retired from the game.

After giving up the frantic pace of the hockey life spent on the road, King settled down with his wife and started a family.

Stats

Season	Team	Games Played	Goals	Assists	Points	Penalties
1973–74	California Golden Seals	2	0	0	0	0
1974–75	California Golden Seals	25	4	7	11	8
1975–76	California Golden Seals	46	1	11	12	26
NHL Totals		73	5	18	23	34

Sandy McCarthy

NEVER ONE TO SHY AWAY from a scrap, Sandy McCarthy knew he was a fighter, and he accepted that role. From his days in the Quebec Major Junior League to his finals days in a New York Rangers uniform, McCarthy's fists were his NHL ticket.

Born in the Toronto area in 1972, McCarthy is of both black and Native descent. As a big teenager, he fully embraced the role of a power forward early on in his career. He began playing hockey in the Georgian Bay Junior C Hockey with the Midland Centennials but eventually moved on to the Quebec Major Junior Hockey League with the Laval Titans in 1989, where he joined fellow Native and tough guy Gino Odjick. McCarthy, Odjick, Michel Gingras and Claude

Boivin were a quartet of bruisers on the Titan squad that made them a formidable opponent to play against.

In McCarthy's first season he scored just 10 goals but racked up 269 minutes in penalties. The following season his points total rose but so did his minutes in the box. By his third season in the "Q" (as the QMJHL is commonly called), he had all the potential of an NHL star power forward, already proving it in his last year in the "Q" with 39 goals and 51 assists. But it was also the 326 minutes in penalties that made him unique. So unique that the Calgary Flames had to have him on their team and drafted him 52nd overall at the 1991 NHL Entry Draft.

McCarthy spent his first five seasons in the NHL with the Flames. He was a valuable member of the team when he played a full season, but many times he was forced out of half the season or more with injuries.

After a bad start in the 1997–98 season, the Flames felt it was time to make some changes. With a missed playoff in 1997, the Flames were looking for a new direction and wanted to add some offense to their lineup. McCarthy was packaged off with their third- and fifth-round choice to the Tampa Bay Lightning in return for Jason Weimer. Calgary's new acquisition did not perform much better than McCarthy, however, and the Flames added insult to injury by giving away their third-round pick, which the Lightning used to select Brad Richards. (Richards went on to help Tampa Bay win the Stanley Cup and take home the Conn Smythe Trophy in 2004.) After one season in Tampa Bay, McCarthy was traded to the Philadelphia Flyers, where he lasted just a half season before again packing his bags, this time landing with the Carolina Hurricanes. He barely had time to unpack his gear before the Hurricanes traded him at the end of the 1999–2000 season to the New York Rangers. The Rangers were looking for some toughness, and the journeyman hockey player finally found a home.

Under the coaching of Ron Low, and placed beside Mark Messier and Petr Nedved, McCarthy flourished, scoring a career-high 11 goals and 23 points. But despite the additional toughness, the New York Rangers still failed to make the playoffs for the three years McCarthy was with them. After the 2002–03 season, he signed with the Boston Bruins as a free agent during the off-season, but he only got to play in 37 games before he was placed on waivers, at which time the Rangers picked him up again for the remainder of the 2003–04 season.

After the NHL lockout season of 2004–05, when the teams returned to action they were looking for a faster and more streamlined scoring team, and McCarthy's brand of "rock 'em, sock 'em" hockey was not wanted any longer in the NHL. The Rangers did not pick up his contract, and no one seemed interested in a big fighter. McCarthy played his last NHL game in 2004.

Stats

Season	Team	Games Played	Goals	Assists	Points	Penalties
1993–94	Calgary Flames	79	5	5	10	173
1994–95	Calgary Flames	37	5	3	8	101
1995–96	Calgary Flames	75	9	7	16	173
1996–97	Calgary Flames	33	3	5	8	113
1997–98	Calgary Flames	52	8	5	13	170
	Tampa Bay Lightning	14	0	5	5	71
1998–99	Tampa Bay Lightning	67	5	7	12	135
	Philadelphia Flyers	13	0	1	1	25
1999–2000	Philadelphia Flyers	58	6	5	11	111
	Carolina Hurricanes	13	0	0	0	9
2000–01	New York Rangers	81	11	10	21	171
2001–02	New York Rangers	82	10	13	23	171
2002–03	New York Rangers	82	6	9	15	81
2003–04	Boston Bruins	37	3	1	4	28
	New York Rangers	13	1	0	1	2
NHL Totals		736	72	76	148	1534

Dale McCourt

BEING RELATED TO ONE of the most famous Native American hockey players ever in the NHL was not the easiest thing to live up to, but Dale McCourt managed to make a pretty good name for himself in NHL history books.

Nephew of the great Toronto Maple Leaf George Armstrong, McCourt, who is one-eighth Ojibway, had one of the best mentors possible growing up. Watching the exploits of his famous uncle every Saturday night gave him the inspiration he needed as a young man to pursue his dream of breaking into the NHL.

In his hometown of Falconbridge, Ontario, Dale's father first introduced him to the game. Every year when the air began to get colder and the ground was blanketed white, the senior McCourt would get out the hose and build a rink for his family of six children. It was on that rink that the young Dale McCourt honed his skills and pretended he was his uncle winning the Stanley Cup.

McCourt graduated from the backyard rink to the arena rather quickly, and by his late teens he got his first real hockey job playing in the Ontario Hockey League (OHL) with the Sudbury Wolves in the 1972–73 season. Playing with the Wolves gave him the experience he needed to play hockey at a higher level, but he still wasn't playing up to his potential. It was when he moved on to the Hamilton Fincups of the OHL that the center's points production soared. McCourt went from 20 goals in the 1973–74 season to 60 goals in his last year in the minors. With point totals like that, it wasn't likely that the NHL clubs would pass him by at the 1977 NHL Amateur Draft.

The Detroit Red Wings were in desperate need of a scoring forward in the late '70s, having spent much of the decade as the league's whipping boys and being unable to rekindle any of the past glory that had been so synonymous with the Red Wings. The Wings were so impressed with McCourt on and off the ice that they used their number-one pick overall to secure him.

Not wanting their new young talent to suffer down in the minors, the Red Wings threw

McCourt into the lion's den for the start of his first NHL season in 1977–78, and he hit the ground running. In his rookie season he scored an incredible 33 goals and added 39 assists, which placed him second among rookies in scoring that year behind Mike Bossy. The Red Wings also had a dramatic change of fortunes—they went from the bottom of their division into second place the following year with McCourt in the lineup.

It was during the off-season after the Wings were eliminated in the playoffs by the Montreal Canadiens that McCourt became involved in a legal battle with the NHL and the Wings management. For some strange reason, after scoring 33 goals in his rookie season, the Red Wings wanted to assign McCourt to the Los Angeles Kings as compensation for allowing the Wings to procure free-agent goaltender Rogie Vachon. After having such a successful rookie season, McCourt strongly opposed being shipped off to the Kings as mere compensation, and he sued the NHL to block the transfer. McCourt received a court order barring the transfer and played three more seasons with the Wings, where he scored an average of 30 goals each year. But the Wings still wanted to get rid of the talented young center, and in the middle of the 1981–82 season they packaged McCourt with a young Mike Foligno and shipped them to the Buffalo Sabres.

Playing two seasons with the Sabres, McCourt managed only two 20-goal seasons. With his production in decline, the Sabres released him at the start of the 1983–84 season, at which time his uncle's old team the Toronto Maple Leafs quickly picked him up. Although he had a decent season with 19 goals and 24 assists, McCourt's time in the NHL came to an end. But with hockey still in his blood, he played for a few more years in the Swiss L'Associazione with the Ambri-Piotta team.

Stats

Season	Team	Games Played	Goals	Assists	Points	Penalties
1977–78	Detroit Red Wings	76	33	39	72	10
1978–79	Detroit Red Wings	79	28	43	71	14
1979–80	Detroit Red Wings	80	30	51	81	12
1980–81	Detroit Red Wings	80	30	56	86	50
1981–82	Detroit Red Wings	26	13	14	27	6
	Buffalo Sabres	52	20	22	42	12
1982–83	Buffalo Sabres	62	20	32	52	10
1983–84	Buffalo Sabres	5	1	3	4	0
	Toronto Maple Leafs	72	19	24	43	10
NHL Totals		532	194	284	478	124

Vic
Mercredi

BORN IN YELLOWKNIFE IN 1953, there was not much else for Vic Mercredi to do in the small community but play hockey. He played for several years in junior leagues around Canada, for the New Westminster Bruins of the Western Canada Hockey League and the Omaha Knights of the Canadian Hockey League, before finally getting his shot at the NHL when the Atlanta Flames drafted him 16th overall at the 1973 NHL Amateur Draft.

But Mercredi's hopes of a long career were dashed as his NHL life lasted only two games. He spent the next few years hopping around pro and semi-pro leagues before giving up hockey in 1979.

Stats

Season		Team	Games Played	Goals	Assists	Points	Penalties
1974–75		Atlanta Flames	2	0	0	0	0
NHL Totals			2	0	0	0	0

Jim
Neilson

ONE LOOK AT JIM NEILSON and you can see the Native ancestry written on his face, but like many of his generation, he grew up without any knowledge of his culture.

Born to a Danish father and a Cree mother, Jim was placed in the St. Patrick's Catholic Orphanage in Prince Albert, Saskatchewan, at a young age. Raised among mainly white orphans, Jim was not taught anything about his people or where he came from, and he spent the majority of his early years without any knowledge of who he was and without connection to his culture.

Despite the absence of his birth family, the orphanage was actually a positive experience for Jim, because it was during his 12 years at St. Patrick's that he was introduced to hockey, something that might not have occurred had he lived on a reserve.

Neilson took to hockey quickly and found out that he played best when on defense. His path to the NHL began in 1959 when he joined the Prince Albert Mintos of the Saskatchewan Junior Hockey League. At 6 feet 1 inch, and 205 pounds, Neilson might have been pigeonholed into the role of an enforcer like many other hockey players his size, but he preferred to let his defensive skill do the talking. That is not to say that he would back away from a scrap, but he preferred to concentrate on the game, and that philosophy served him well.

Neilson made the leap to the professional ranks in 1961 when he joined the Kitchener-Waterloo Beavers of the Eastern Professional Hockey League. Expecting to be in the minor ranks for a few more years before the NHL would even begin to look at him, Neilson received the surprise of his life when after only one season with the Beavers he was scouted and signed to the New York Rangers.

"My hockey career took off very fast. I still had a year of junior left when I went to the Rangers camp in New York," said Neilson in the book *They Call Me Chief.*

> "It just happened so fast! I was lucky because the Rangers weren't a very good team at the time; well, we had good players but it was

the six-team NHL and there were some out-standing teams which kept us and the Bruins out of the four-team playoffs. I was just good enough at that early age to stick with the starting roster. But a good year with the Kitchener-Waterloo Beavers doesn't even come close to your experience with the New York Rangers. All of a sudden, you're playing defense against the Howes and the Beliveaus!"

And Neilson was exactly what the Rangers needed at the time to fend off the power forwards of the league at the time. Never one to venture too far from his duties, as a big stay-at-home defenseman, Neilson could tie up the players at the blue line and make them think twice before trying it again.

Playing during the same years as arguably the most famous Native hockey player, Toronto Maple Leaf George Armstrong, Neilson was aware of Armstrong's presence in the league and knew of his reputation. As the two biggest Native hockey players in the NHL, they were given nicknames to match. George Armstrong had always been known as "The Chief," and Neilson was given the lesser name of the "Up-and-Coming Chief."

The strange thing about such a nickname for most Native hockey players is that when coming from teammates, they know it is in good nature, but when used by opponents, the name takes on a whole new connotation. Being a Native hockey player in the NHL in the '60s wasn't always easy, and racism was something the players had to endure.

"Hockey is a tough game, and professional hockey is so competitive…it's a fight to the death to keep your job…the pressure…But to sink to that level of insulting somebody because of their race… you are insulting the children, the innocent children, the women, the good people of that race," said Neilson.

The racism bothered Neilson, but his calm demeanor and good nature kept him out of the penalty box and probably added several years to his hockey career. He played defense for the Rangers for 12 years and then was claimed by the California Golden Seals in the Intra-League Draft in 1974. He finished out his NHL career with the Cleveland Barons in 1978.

Jim Neilson never won a Stanley Cup or any trophies, but he was the type of player every coach wanted on his team—someone who had a positive attitude and a work ethic to match.

Stats

Season	Team	Games Played	Goals	Assists	Points	Penalties
1962–63	New York Rangers	69	5	11	16	38
1963–64	New York Rangers	69	5	24	29	93
1964–65	New York Rangers	62	0	13	13	58
1965–66	New York Rangers	65	4	19	23	84
1966–67	New York Rangers	61	4	11	15	65
1967–68	New York Rangers	67	6	29	35	60
1968–69	New York Rangers	76	10	34	44	95
1969–70	New York Rangers	62	3	20	23	75
1970–71	New York Rangers	77	8	24	32	69
1971–72	New York Rangers	78	7	30	37	56
1972–73	New York Rangers	52	4	16	20	35
1973–74	New York Rangers	72	4	7	11	38
1974–75	California Golden Seals	72	3	17	20	56
1975–76	California Golden Seals	26	1	6	7	20
1976–77	Cleveland Barons	47	3	17	20	42
1977–78	Cleveland Barons	68	2	21	23	20
NHL Totals		1023	69	299	368	904

Ted
Nolan

ALTHOUGH THEODORE JOHN NOLAN played several years in the NHL, it is his career as a coach for which he is best known.

Born on the Garden River First Nations Reserve in northwestern Ontario in 1958, Ted Nolan, a full-blooded Ojibway, did not have many opportunities as a child. Nolan grew up in an impoverished community, where many, including Nolan, lived in homes without indoor plumbing or electricity. Drug and alcohol abuse abounded, and most of the people were jobless. This was not the ideal environment for any child to grow up in, but Nolan had a strong mother who instilled in him from a young age a sense of pride and courage that would serve him well growing up in a country that looked down on his people.

Despite the conditions he found himself in, Nolan made the best of what he was given. Learning to play hockey with second-hand equipment, he started out playing hockey on local teams and with some hard work and a few sacrifices, he made his way into the junior hockey ranks playing for teams in Kenora and Sault Ste. Marie. Although not blessed with the natural talent of a scoring forward, Nolan made up for any deficiencies with an incredible work ethic.

All the hard work paid off when the Detroit Red Wings selected him 78th overall at the 1978 NHL Amateur Draft. He spent the next three seasons in the club's minor league affiliate, the Adirondack Red Wings of the American Hockey League, before finally getting the call halfway through the 1981–82 season to play in the big leagues.

In his first season with the Red Wings, Nolan only managed to score four goals and 13 assists in 41 games, not the type of stats that would keep a player in the NHL for very long if they had nothing else to offer. He was sent back down to the minors for another year of conditioning before he again got the call to the NHL. This time his stay was even shorter. After just 19 games and one goal, the Detroit Red Wings had had their fill of Nolan and released him from his contract. The Buffalo Sabres signed him as a free agent, but he never got to play for them as his rights were almost immediately shipped off to the Pittsburgh Penguins.

It was with Pittsburgh that Nolan hoped to turn things around. They were a young team and needed a grinding hockey player like Nolan to complement the play of the scoring forwards like the young Mario Lemieux. But things did not work out the way Nolan had hoped. After just 18 games he suffered a debilitating back injury that forced him into early retirement. But he didn't stay away from hockey for long. To leave the game that had given him so much was not an option for Nolan, and he quickly turned to coaching.

Just two years after leaving the NHL, Nolan joined his old team, the Sault Ste. Marie Greyhounds, in the middle of the 1988–89 season when the other head coach was let go for leading the team to the worst record in the league. Two years later, the team's fortunes completely reversed, thanks to Nolan. Under his tenure, the Greyhounds won three con- secutive Ontario Hockey Association league championships.

Nolan was so successful that the NHL began to take notice, and in 1994 he was hired as the assis- tant coach of the Hartford Whalers under head coach Paul Holmgren. One year later, Nolan was hired by the Buffalo Sabres as their new head coach for the start of the 1995–96 season.

When he arrived on the scene in 1995, the team consisted basically of two superstars and a group of hardworking, grunt-type players. Nolan had come from his minor league coaching duties with the theory that if you worked as a team, you won as a team, and that there was no proverbial "I" on his bench. The only problem was that he had goal-tender Dominik Hasek on his team, and from the beginning, the two individuals never saw eye to eye.

The relationship between Nolan and Hasek remained rocky despite the Sabres' dramatic turn-around during the 1996–97 season, where they rocketed to the top of their division.

Nolan even won the Jack Adams Trophy as Coach of the Year and looked to be securing a long future as an NHL coach, but then came the 1997 playoffs, and everything began to fall apart.

In game three of the first round against Ottawa, Hasek felt a pop in his knee and pulled himself out of the game after letting in a goal. That is when rumors began to circulate that Hasek had bailed on his team, and reporter Jim Kelley took it upon himself to call Hasek out in the press for his "desertion" and for his open dislike of the Buffalo head coach. Tensions were running so high that after the Sabres lost game five of the series to Ottawa, Hasek came out of the dressing room and physically attacked Kelley. Things only deteriorated from that point on.

After backup goaltender Steve Shields put in the performance of his career to help lift the Sabres past the Senators in game seven, the NHL announced that, healthy or not, Hasek would be suspended for three games for his attack on Kelley.

Up against a tough Philadelphia Flyers squad, the Sabres could have used Hasek in nets, but the task was left up to Shields to hold down the fort. But a backup goaltender could only do so much. Nolan's Sabres fell behind three games to none, and everyone was just waiting for Hasek to return so that he might help them turn things in their favor. But Hasek again declared himself unfit to play, and the Sabres were eliminated in five games by the Flyers.

As strained as Nolan's relationship with Hasek was, it was equally so with general manager John Muckler. What made the situation even worse for Nolan was that the superstar and the general manager teamed up to push him out of his job for good. Just two years into his dream job as head coach of an NHL franchise, Nolan was fired. It seemed like a ridiculous firing since he had turned the franchise around and won the coach of the year honors, but politics and hockey never mix, and Nolan got caught in the middle of a classic power struggle.

After losing the position, Nolan turned his focus back to the community he loved and became a representative of the Assembly of First Nations. He traveled across North America giving motivational speeches to impressionable young Aboriginals and helped in establishing hockey programs for Native youths.

It was eight years before Nolan returned to his position behind the bench, but this time it wasn't in the NHL. He was back in the minor league system as head coach of the Quebec Major Junior League's Moncton Wildcats. He led the Wildcats all the way to the Memorial Cup final against the Quebec Ramparts. The Wildcats lost the final to former NHL goaltender Patrick Roy's Quebec Ramparts. However, Nolan had sent out the signal to the NHL that he was ready to return to the professional ranks of coaching.

The New York Islanders needed a tough coach who had a proven ability to pull a struggling young team into the win column, and Nolan, despite his earlier controversies, had proven himself quite capable of handling the task.

In the 2005–06 season the Islanders were a struggling team that needed direction. They did not have any leadership behind the bench, having had two coaches in one season, and their record showed their lack of direction. Then Ted Nolan arrived on the scene for the start of the 2006–07 season and turned the Islanders' fortunes around. They finished the season with a winning record and just made it into the playoffs.

And wouldn't you know it, Nolan's first-round opponents were his old team, the Buffalo Sabres. But the Sabres of 2007 were just too dominant a force for the Islanders to handle, and Nolan's team succumbed in just five games.

After a disappointing season in 2007–08, Nolan was once again put out of a job when he was fired after the Islanders missed the playoffs. Nolan for his part returned to his home on the reserve he grew up on and continues with his charity work.

Stats

Season	Team	Games Played	Goals	Assists	Points	Penalties
1981–82	Detroit Red Wings	41	4	13	17	45
1983–84	Detroit Red Wings	19	1	2	3	26
1985–86	Pittsburgh Penguins	18	1	1	2	34
NHL Totals		78	6	16	22	105

Gino
Odjick

WAYNE GINO ODJICK, also known as the "Algonquin Enforcer," was born on the Kitigan Zibi Anishinabeg Reserve near Maniwaki, Quebec. From the moment he put on skates, there was no allusion that Gino would be the next Bryan Trottier. Gino was a tough guy, and he fully accepted that role and knew it was his ticket into the NHL.

He started his journey to the big leagues in the Quebec Major Junior Hockey League with the Laval Titans, and from the outset Odjick was the enforcer. But what set him apart from most other "fighters" was that he could actually play the game well. He didn't score much, but he functioned as a calming agent whenever he was on the ice, meaning that the other team didn't dare bother his teammates

when he was on the ice or there would be conse-
quences. And he was not bad defensively either.

In two seasons with the Laval Titans, Odjick
racked up just 21 goals but had a whopping
558 minutes in penalties. Despite his lack of goal
production as a left wing, his particular talent in
the fisticuffs department was an asset when it came
time for the 1990 NHL Entry Draft. He was drafted
in the fifth round, 86th overall, by the Vancouver
Canucks, who needed some muscle to match up
against the division rivals of Los Angeles, Calgary
and Edmonton.

Odjick was sent down to the club's junior team for
further conditioning at the start of the 1990–91 season but was called up to the pros after only playing
in 17 games. Vancouver needed a player who could
protect its stars, and they found the perfect one in
Gino Odjick. In his first 45 games he scored seven
goals and managed 296 minutes in penalties.

In his time with the Canucks, Odjick had some
memorable games. One game stands out, among
many, when Odjick decided to take on the entire
St. Louis Blues. During the course of that particular game, a melee occurred on the ice, and Odjick
was at the center of it all. Moving from one guy to
the next, Odjick tried to fight every Blues player he
could get his hands on, skating around the ice looking for his next opponent. The linesmen tried to

stop him, but Odjick just skated away or got involved in another fight. At one point he tried to take on Blues forward Glenn Anderson, but the veteran just skated away from the now shirtless Odjick. Two linesmen had to step in to remove him from the ice to restore order to the game.

Odjick played eight seasons with the Canucks before he was traded to the New York Islanders in 1997. He played three seasons with the Islanders before bouncing around to the Philadelphia Flyers and finally ending up with the Montreal Canadiens.

While he was with the Flyers, injuries from fighting his way through his hockey career began to take their toll, and Odjick never played more than 40 games in one season. The last season of his career came in 2001–02 with the Montreal Canadiens.

In 2003 Odjick moved back to Vancouver and remains actively involved in community affairs, as well as being part owner of the Musqueam Golf and Learning Academy.

Stats

Season	Team	Games Played	Goals	Assists	Points	Penalties
1990–91	Vancouver Canucks	45	7	1	8	296
1991–92	Vancouver Canucks	65	4	6	10	348
1992–93	Vancouver Canucks	75	4	13	17	370
1993–94	Vancouver Canucks	76	16	13	29	271
1994–95	Vancouver Canucks	23	4	5	9	109
1995–96	Vancouver Canucks	55	3	4	7	181
1996–97	Vancouver Canucks	70	5	8	13	371
1997–98	Vancouver Canucks	35	3	2	5	181
	New York Islanders	13	0	0	0	31
1998–99	New York Islanders	23	4	3	7	133
1999–2000	New York Islanders	46	5	10	15	30
	Philadelphia Flyers	13	3	1	4	10
2000–01	Philadelphia Flyers	17	1	3	4	28
	Montreal Canadiens	13	1	0	1	44
2001–02	Montreal Canadiens	36	4	4	8	104
NHL Totals		605	64	73	137	2567

Everett Sanipass

THE MI'KMAQ PEOPLE HAVE BEEN playing a form of hockey for centuries, so it was no surprise to see their own Everett Sanipass flourish in the sport from an early age.

The Big Cove, New Brunswick native first began to turn heads on the ice when he played for the Moncton Flyers of the New Brunswick Amateur Hockey Association in 1983–84. That season he scored 43 goals in 37 games and was well on his way to developing into a slick, scoring forward. But like so many Native hockey players, he was pigeonholed into the role of a fighter by the time he reached the junior ranks.

Despite his time on the ice being devoted to fighting, Sanipass still managed to score a respectable 28 goals and 66 assists in his second year with

the Verdun Junior Canadiens in 1985–86. His toughness and scoring ability were exactly what the
Chicago Blackhawks were looking for when they
drafted him 14th overall at the 1986 NHL Entry Draft.
He was also noticed by Hockey Canada and asked
to join the junior national team for the 1987 World
Junior Championship in Piestany, Czechoslovakia.
The tournament ended up being one of Sanipass'
most memorable career moments.

Ever since the Russians became players in international hockey, they have had a contentious
relationship with Canada. Through the Olympic
years to the 1972 Summit Series, those tensions rose
to the surface for one game between the Canadian
and the Soviet juniors.

When the two teams met, the Soviets were out of
medal contention and had absolutely nothing to lose
in the game. Canada needed to beat the Soviets by
five goals to be assured a gold medal, any less
would be silver, and a bronze was already theirs
for the taking. It was 4–2 in the middle of the second period when all hell broke loose on the ice.

Most reports afterwards said that the alterca-
tion began when a Russian player sucker punched
Theoren Fleury without provocation, but Fleury
remembers that it all started because of Sanipass.

In the corner of the rink, Fleury noticed that
a Soviet player was on top of Sanipass, so Fleury

decided to get back at the Soviet player for messing with his teammate and punched him in the face. That's when both benches cleared and everyone started fighting. The officials on the ice could do little to break up the fight and simply left the ice. When order was restored, both teams were kicked out of the tournament, and Canada returned home empty-handed. The brawl was the subject of much discussion weeks after it happened. It even got its own name: "The Punch-up in Piestany."

Shortly after his experience at the World Junior Championships, Sanipass got his start in the big leagues at the end of the Blackhawks' 1986–87 season. He played in just seven games but managed to score his first NHL goal. He played two more seasons in Chicago, getting a season-high eight goals. The Blackhawks traded him to the Quebec Nordiques in 1990, but Sanipass was plagued by constant back problems and never played more than 40 games with the Nordiques in two seasons. He ended up bouncing around the minor leagues before spinal surgery ended his playing career.

Had he been healthy and focused more on his natural talent, things might have turned out better in the long run for Sanipass. After retiring from hockey, he returned to his home province of New Brunswick where he got a job with the Canadian government.

Stats

Season	Team	Games Played	Goals	Assists	Points	Penalties
1986–87	Chicago Blackhawks	7	1	3	4	2
1987–88	Chicago Blackhawks	57	8	12	20	126
1988–89	Chicago Blackhawks	50	6	9	15	164
1989–90	Chicago Blackhawks	12	2	2	4	17
	Quebec Nordiques	9	3	3	6	8
1990–91	Quebec Nordiques	29	5	5	10	41
NHL Totals		164	25	34	59	358

Bobby Simpson

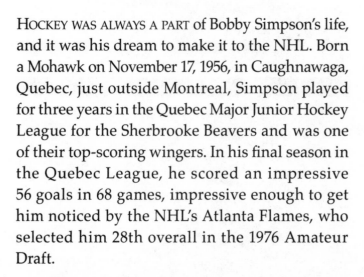

HOCKEY WAS ALWAYS A PART of Bobby Simpson's life, and it was his dream to make it to the NHL. Born a Mohawk on November 17, 1956, in Caughnawaga, Quebec, just outside Montreal, Simpson played for three years in the Quebec Major Junior Hockey League for the Sherbrooke Beavers and was one of their top-scoring wingers. In his final season in the Quebec League, he scored an impressive 56 goals in 68 games, impressive enough to get him noticed by the NHL's Atlanta Flames, who selected him 28th overall in the 1976 Amateur Draft.

But Simpson's time in the NHL was not as fruitful as his junior career; he never managed to secure a full-time position. He spent two seasons with the Atlanta Flames before moving to the

St. Louis Blues in 1980 and then to the Pittsburgh Penguins in 1982. He was the prototype hockey journeyman, bouncing around from team to team and league to league, always looking for that next shot at the big show. Simpson played his last NHL game with the Penguins in 1983 and never made it back.

Stats

Season	Team	Games Played	Goals	Assists	Points	Penalties
1976–77	Atlanta Flames	72	13	10	23	45
1977–78	Atlanta Flames	55	10	8	18	49
1979–80	St. Louis Blues	18	2	2	4	0
1981–82	Pittsburgh Penguins	26	9	9	18	4
1982–83	Pittsburgh Penguins	4	1	0	1	0
NHL Totals		175	35	29	64	98

Frank
St. Marseille

OF MÉTIS HERITAGE, Frank St. Marseille was born in Levack, Ontario, in 1939. He got his start in the NHL relatively late in life, only making it to the big leagues at the age of 28. It wasn't because he was a bad hockey player, it was that when he was in his late teens, the NHL had only six teams and getting in was not easy.

But when the league expanded in 1967, St. Marseille finally got his chance with the St. Louis Blues. Although he was placed on an expansion team that had little hope of success, he was coached by young Scotty Bowman, the coach who went on to become one of the most successful coaches in NHL history. And because all the expansion teams were placed in the West Division while the original six stayed in the east, it ensured that the Blues would not have to face any eastern teams until the final round of the playoffs. All they had to do was win their division, and they did so in 1968, 1969 and in 1970. Unfortunately, each time they got to the Stanley Cup final they were met by either the Montreal Canadiens or the Boston Bruins and had no hope of winning the series (which they didn't).

St. Marseille was a good second- and third-line right wing who always showed up to each game ready to work hard and contribute to the team. He maintained a decent scoring pace throughout much of his career, never hitting the 20-goal plateau but staying consistently in that range.

By 1973 the Blues wanted to move in a different direction and traded St. Marseille to the Los Angeles Kings. He played another four years in the NHL, leaving the Kings and the NHL at the end of the 1976–77 season.

In total, St. Marseille played 707 NHL games, scoring 140 goals and 285 assists, and he also played in 88 playoff games.

He might not have been a star player, but in the NHL sometimes a consistent player is much more valued than a flash-in-the-pan goal scorer.

Stats

Season	Team	Games Played	Goals	Assists	Points	Penalties
1967–68	St. Louis Blues	57	16	16	32	12
1968–69	St. Louis Blues	72	12	26	38	22
1969–70	St. Louis Blues	74	16	43	59	18
1970–71	St. Louis Blues	77	19	32	51	26
1971–72	St. Louis Blues	78	16	36	52	32
1972–73	St. Louis Blues	45	7	18	25	8
	Los Angeles Kings	29	7	4	11	2
1973–74	Los Angeles Kings	78	14	36	50	40
1974–75	Los Angeles Kings	80	17	36	53	46
1975–76	Los Angeles Kings	68	10	16	26	20
1976–77	Los Angeles Kings	49	6	22	28	16
. NHL Totals		707	140	285	425	242

Bryan Trottier

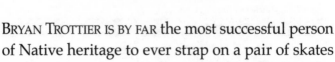

BRYAN TROTTIER IS BY FAR the most successful person of Native heritage to ever strap on a pair of skates in the NHL. His name has been engraved on the Stanley Cup six times: as a player and as assistant coach of the Colorado Avalanche. Trottier was the second Native American recipient of the Conn Smythe Trophy as the playoffs' most valuable player when he won it in 1980. (Reggie Leach had won it in 1976 with the Philadelphia Flyers.)

Born in the small town of Val Marie, Saskatchewan, in 1956, Bryan was the son of an Irish mother and a Métis father. Bryan's first love in life was not hockey but rodeo. Although he was born in Canada, his family moved to the central U.S. for his father's construction job. It was there that the young Trottier grew to love horses and the excitement of the rodeo. But when Bryan was six, the Trottiers moved back to the family ranch in Val Marie, where Bryan discovered a new game that all the kids in the area were playing.

Every winter, Bryan could be found on the frozen river not too far from his house skating up and down with a stick and puck, working on his technique. Soon he was good enough to join an organized hockey league and began starring with the Prince Albert Raiders and the Swift Current Broncos of the Western Junior Hockey League in the early 1970s.

Away from his family much of the year traveling through the small towns of Canada on the hockey circuit, Trottier found hockey life a little lonely. His parents were not wealthy and his family was large, so it was never easy to bring the entire family to see his games, but on occasion they did make it out. However, in order to afford the hotel, food and tickets, the family needed a supplemental source of income. The Trottier family had always been musical, so when they traveled to different towns to see their son play hockey, the entire family took along their instruments and played in the local bars and restaurants in order to finance the trip. After a game, Trottier would occasionally play bass in the band, while his teammates boozed it up at some club.

This sense of family was important to Trottier; it served him well on those lonely nights on the road and kept him out of trouble.

Focused on his hockey career, Trottier scored 46 goals in 67 games in his final year in the junior leagues in 1974–75. During the summer of 1975 at the NHL Amateur Draft, the New York Islanders selected Trottier 22nd overall and immediately signed him to the team. He premiered with the Islanders for the 1975–76 season and played in all 80 games, scoring 32 goals and 63 assists. His exploits on the ice earned him the NHL's Rookie of the Year honors, and he became the first Native player to win the Calder Trophy. Things only got better for him from that point on.

In the 1978–79 season, Trottier's 47 goals and 87 assists were good enough to win him the Art Ross Trophy as the NHL's leading scorer and the Hart Trophy as the league's Most Valuable Player. That year the Islanders were taken out of the playoff semi-finals by their hated rivals, the New York Rangers, but with a team of players consisting of Mike Bossy, Denis Potvin, Bryan Trottier and others, the Islanders could not be held back for long. The 1980s saw the death of the stranglehold the original six teams had on the Stanley Cup with the rise of a new dynasty, the New York Islanders.

During the 1979–80 season the Islanders were not the best team in the league. They were more than 20 points behind the league-leading Philadelphia Flyers and were not among the favorites to make it to the finals. But as the common saying in hockey goes, the playoffs are an entirely new season. What happened in the regular season was set aside, and the New York Islanders made it to the finals against the Flyers and won the Cup.

Trottier went on to lead the Islanders to four consecutive Stanley Cups. Although Wayne Gretzky eventually entered the league and completely dominated the scoreboard, it was Bryan Trottier who was considered the best all-round player. He could score like Gretzky, but he also was one of the best defensive forwards in the game. He could give and take a body check with the toughest in the league and was the leader on the Islanders' special teams.

In terms of goals, Trottier's best season was in 1981–82 when he hit the magical 50-goal mark, becoming the first Native player to do so. (Only Jonathan Cheechoo has scored more, 56 goals in the 2005–06 season with the San Jose Sharks.)

Trottier almost took the Islanders to an unprecedented fifth straight Stanley Cup during the 1983–84 season, but Gretzky and the Edmonton Oilers stopped him.

Apart from his duties in the NHL, Trottier also took every chance he could to compete internationally. In the 1980s, because NHL players were not allowed in the Winter Olympics, the only tournament to measure national hockey superiority was the Canada Cup. Since its inception, the Canada Cup had been the premiere world hockey tournament, and there was no doubt that in 1984 Bryan Trottier was one of the premiere players in the NHL. It was only natural that most Canadians expected him to play on their side, but when Trottier agreed to play with the Americans, he was demonized somewhat in the Canadian press. But the choice was his, something he was given the rights to do by virtue of being born Native, and no one was going to tell him different. As a Native American, he was allowed to travel across the borders without hassle and had the privilege of duel citizenship.

"It wasn't a very popular decision. But I felt very strongly that I wanted to give something back to the country I was making my living in," said Trottier. "Plus, there was also a little stubborn side that, when the Committee said you can't do this, I said, 'I'm a North American Indian and Yes! I can!'"

Canada ended up winning the tournament, beating Sweden in the finals.

Trottier continued to play solid hockey throughout the '80s, but the team around him was not the same anymore. Mike Bossy was slowing down and eventually had to retire because of an injury, Denis Potvin was still effective but getting older, and goaltender Billy Smith just didn't play with that same fire he did back in the early '80s.

Eventually, age began catching up to Trottier as well, and his effectiveness on the ice began to suffer. The NHL was changing, and the new players were bigger, faster and a lot tougher. It wasn't a league for old guys under six feet tall. But Trottier felt he could still contribute on the defensive end and, more importantly, as a veteran leader on a young team. In 1990 the Islanders traded Trottier to the Pittsburgh Penguins, and in his first year his wisdom and winning ways seemed to rub off on the team as they won the 1991 Stanley Cup and followed it up with another in the 1992.

For all those who had written him off as a old man, it was with great pride that Trottier held those two Stanley Cups up high in the '90s. But at 36 years of age, "Trots," as his teammates called him (not "Chief"), was at the end of his career. After the 1993–94 season he finally called it quits. In his 18 years as a professional hockey player, Bryan Trottier had scored 524 goals and 901 assists in 1279 games.

But the lure of the game and all that surrounded it still resounded in Trottier, and he moved straight from the ice to behind the bench as the Penguins' assistant coach. He stayed with the team through to the end of the 1996–97 season when he left Pittsburgh to become the head coach of the Portland Pirates of the American Hockey League. He wanted to gain some practical experience as a leader behind the bench to hopefully return to the NHL to lead a team of his own.

Trottier returned to the NHL in 1997–98 as an assistant with the Colorado Avalanche, who went on to win the Cup in 2001. It seemed that everything he touched turned to Stanley, and in 2002 the New York Rangers were hoping some of that luck would rub off on their squad of overpaid talent and hired Trottier as their head coach. But he wasn't given much of a chance to turn things around as he was fired mid-season because of the team's losing record.

Despite the shot to his pride at having been fired, Trottier did not stay away from hockey for long, and in 2006 he returned to the New York Islanders as executive director of play personnel. Now only if some of that magic will once again rub off on the Islanders.

Stats

Season	Team	Games Played	Goals	Assists	Points	Penalties
1975–76	New York Islanders	80	32	63	95	21
1976–77	New York Islanders	76	30	42	72	34
1977–78	New York Islanders	77	46	77	123	46
1978–79	New York Islanders	76	47	87	134	50
1979–80	New York Islanders	78	42	62	104	68
1980–81	New York Islanders	73	31	72	103	74
1981–82	New York Islanders	80	50	79	129	88
1982–83	New York Islanders	80	34	55	89	68
1983–84	New York Islanders	68	40	71	111	59
1984–85	New York Islanders	68	28	31	59	47
1985–86	New York Islanders	78	37	59	96	72
1986–87	New York Islanders	80	23	64	87	50
1987–88	New York Islanders	77	30	52	82	48
1988–89	New York Islanders	73	17	28	45	44
1989–90	New York Islanders	59	13	11	24	29
1990–91	Pittsburgh Penguins	52	9	19	28	24
1991–92	Pittsburgh Penguins	63	11	18	29	54
1993–94	Pittsburgh Penguins	41	4	11	15	36
NHL Totals		1279	524	901	1425	912

Chris
Simon

AT ONE POINT IN CHRIS SIMON'S CAREER he was the top goal scorer on his team, a team that included the likes of Peter Bondra and Adam Oates. By his reputation alone, one might not think of Simon as much of a hockey player, but throughout the ups and downs of his career he has been a key part of the teams he has played for, and not just in contributions with his fists.

Born in Wawa, Ontario, in 1972 to an Ojibway father and a white mother, Chris fell victim to alcohol abuse in his teenage years. Fortunately, he had hockey to fall back on, and the game led him away from any major problems, but drinking was an issue that would come back to haunt him through much of his career.

With his hockey career on track, Simon joined up with the Ottawa 67's of the Ontario Hockey League for the 1988–89 season. He didn't have the greatest of rookie seasons, scoring only four goals in 36 games, but the coaching staff liked what they saw and invited him back the next season. It was a good thing they did, because Simon had a breakout 1989–90 season with 36 goals and 38 assists in 57 games. He also racked up 146 minutes in penalties and proved that he could drop the gloves with the best in the league and still contribute to the points on the scoreboard.

Simon was the kind of player who naturally appealed to many teams, but to the Philadelphia Flyers more specifically, and at the 1990 NHL Entry Draft they selected him 25th overall.

After spending two more years in the minor leagues, Simon was looking forward to making his entrance into the professional ranks with the Flyers, but in June 1992 he was thrown into a strange circumstance.

The star player of the 1991 NHL Entry Draft was without a doubt a young man named Eric Lindros. It was no secret who the last place Quebec Nordiques were going to select come draft day, but it was also no secret that the young star did not want to play in such a small-market city. Despite knowing that Lindros did not want to have any part of the Nordiques, they selected him anyway, but Lindros refused to be moved to Quebec. Not wanting to get stuck with an unmotivated player, the Nordiques looked around the league for a buyer, and the Philadelphia Flyers came with the biggest offer. In exchange for Lindros, the Flyers sent Peter Forsberg, Steve Duchene, Kerry Huffman, Mike Ricci, Ron Hextall and, of course, Chris Simon, to the Nordiques. It was a blockbuster trade that eventually led to the franchise winning the Stanley Cup in 1996, but as the Colorado Avalanche.

While with the Nordiques, Simon played sparingly. He never played more than 40 games in one season and was often only put on the ice in an enforcer role. There was no doubt that he was good in the one role the Nordiques required from him, but Simon could actually play hockey if given the space and time. He showed that when the Nordiques franchise folded and moved operations to Colorado. Simon relished the change to Colorado, and it showed on the points sheet. He scored 16 goals, 18 assists and had 250 minutes in penalties in 64 games. He played 12 games in the playoffs and got to raise the Stanley Cup above his head when the Avalanche won it in 1996.

When a team wins the Stanley Cup, each player is awarded 24 hours with the trophy to take it where he pleases. For Simon's time with the Cup, he took it back to his hometown of Wawa, Ontario, and after the town party he put the Cup in a boat and went fishing with his grandfather.

Any hopes of repeating as champions with the Avalanche were dashed when Simon was traded to the Washington Capitals just before the start of the 1996–97 season. His first few years with the Capitals were tough and not without controversy.

During a game against the Edmonton Oilers, Simon and Oilers forward Mike Grier, who is black, got into a pushing match, and Simon apparently called Grier the "N" word. There was some speculation that Grier had made an equally racist remark about Simon's Native heritage, but it could not be confirmed. Despite the lack of evidence or a witness, the NHL suspended Simon for three games while Grier received no reprimand.

With a growing reputation as the league's bad boy, Simon hoped that in the new 1997–98 season he could show the league that he was more than just a fighter and an instigator, and that he could actually score. He started the season off great, with seven goals in 28 games but was forced out for the rest of the season because of a shoulder injury. He did, however, return for the playoffs and provided the physical presence to the Capitals' lineup that helped them get all the way to the Stanley Cup finals. Unfortunately, they lost the series in four straight games to the Detroit Red Wings.

It was a bitter disappointment for Simon to miss most of the season with an injury and then to lose the Cup when he had come so close. He had hoped to return the following season with a strong outing, but once again he was plagued by injury and only ended up playing in 23 games during the 1998–99 season.

He finally had the season he had always wanted in 1999–2000. He played in 75 games, scored 29 goals (team leading) and 20 assists. He played three more seasons with the Capitals before being traded in 2003 to the Chicago Blackhawks. He lasted all of one season with the Hawks before landing with New York Rangers in 2003–04 and then with the Calgary Flames that same year. He got all the way to the finals with Calgary in 2004, but once again his team ended up on the losing end in the Stanley Cup finals (defeated in seven games by the Tampa Bay Lightning).

The 2006–07 season was a controversial one for Simon. At first, when he was traded to the New York Islanders during the off-season, it seemed like the perfect fit. The Islanders were a young team with some scoring potential up front, and they needed a big man who could protect the stars and put in the occasional goal himself. Simon fit the bill to a tee. He had always been a little bit of a hothead during his career, but in putting him under the watchful eye of fellow Native, head coach Ted Nolan, the powers that be thought that he might straighten himself out. But halfway through the season, Simon was involved in an on-ice incident that had the media buzzing for weeks.

On December 15, 2007, in a home game against the Pittsburgh Penguins, the Pens Tim Jackman and uber-pest Jarkko Ruutu exchanged some not-so-kind words with the Islanders bench during a stop in the game. This is when Simon came skating over to the bench and pushed Ruutu to the ground. While Ruutu was on the ice, Simon stepped on the back of his leg with the sharp blade of his skate. The referee spotted this and gave Simon a match penalty for his attempt to injure Ruutu. The next day Simon agreed to go on an indefinite paid leave from the Islanders and "get away from hockey" as he put it. Despite volunteering to leave, the NHL suspended Simon for 30 games. League disciplinarian Colin Campbell said that Simon "had repeatedly evidenced the lack of ability to control his actions" and so merited the 30-game suspension.

A similar incident occurred in March 2008 when Chris Pronger of the Anaheim Ducks stepped on Vancouver Canucks Ryan Kesler's leg. It was exactly the same infraction, but Pronger only received an eight-game suspension. Simon was one of the first to speak up about the related incidents.

"My opinion is there's obviously two sets of rules," Simon told the Minnesota *Pioneer-Press*. "If you look at the tape and look at his history, you can't say we're different, other than he is a star player and I am not."

It was true that the punishments were unfair, but Simon had people talking again after returning from his suspension when the Islanders faced their long-time rivals the New York Rangers in March 2008. The incident in question occurred in the third period as Simon and Rangers forward Ryan Hollweg went into the corner after the puck. As Simon went into the corner, Hollweg crosschecked him from behind, sending Simon headfirst into the boards and giving him what was later diagnosed as a concussion. Play continued, and as Simon slowly got up from the ice he saw Hollweg coming back towards him. Simon then grabbed his stick with both hands and slashed Hollweg across the face, cutting him on the chin. The slash would have been much worse were it not for Hollweg's shoulder pads taking the initial blunt force. For the second time that year Simon was given another suspension, this time for 25 games.

After that incident Chris Simon did not last much longer in the NHL. He played another 30 games with the Islanders in 2007–08 and then was traded to the Minnesota Wild where he only played

10 games. He now plays in the Kontinental Hockey League in Russia for the Chekhov Vityaz.

Say what you will about Simon, but he is a man who always played the game by his rules, never took any dirt from another player, and when he retires he can be assured that his name will be remembered in the history books of hockey.

Stats

Season	Team	Games Played	Goals	Assists	Points	Penalties
1992–93	Quebec Nordiques	16	1	1	2	67
1993–94	Quebec Nordiques	37	4	4	8	132
1994–95	Quebec Nordiques	29	3	9	12	106
1995–96	Colorado Avalanche	64	16	18	34	250
1996–97	Washington Capitals	42	9	13	22	165
1997–98	Washington Capitals	28	7	10	17	38
1998–99	Washington Capitals	23	3	7	10	48
1999–2000	Washington Capitals	75	29	20	49	146
2000–01	Washington Capitals	60	10	10	20	109
2001–02	Washington Capitals	82	14	17	31	137
2002–03	Washington Capitals	10	0	2	2	23
	Chicago Blackhawks	61	12	6	18	125
2003–04	New York Rangers	65	14	9	23	225
	Calgary Flames	13	3	2	5	25
2005–06	Calgary Flames	72	8	14	22	94
2006–07	New York Islanders	67	10	17	27	75
2007–08	New York Islanders	28	1	2	3	43
	Minnesota Wild	10	0	0	0	16
NHL Totals		782	144	161	305	1824

Theoren Fleury

THEOREN WALLACE FLEURY was born in 1968 in the small town of Oxbow, Saskatchewan, to Harry and Jean Fleury. Young Theo was taught to be proud of his Métis heritage, and that sense of pride would serve the diminutive hockey player in his career, but it also led him down a dangerous path.

Hockey was a passion for Fleury from an early age, and throughout his hockey career his abilities were always questioned because of his size. At 5 feet 6 inches, 180 pounds fully developed, Fleury seemed half the size of some of the players coming up through the system at the time. But what Fleury lacked in size, he more than made up for in passion, intensity and sheer talent.

Fleury surprised all detractors when he made the 1984–85 Western Hockey League Moose Jaw Warriors team and scored 29 goals and 46 assists in 71 games. It was his first year in a bigger and faster league, and he still kept up with the best of them. With each progressive year in the WHL, Fleury only got better, and by the 1986–87 season he was the Warriors' leading scorer and top player despite his size disadvantage. Normally, when a player puts up numbers like that he would not stay long in the minors, but because of Fleury's size, he was kept down in the WHL for a full four years.

Even after he was drafted 166th overall in 1987 by the Calgary Flames, the organization kept him with their affiliate club for another two years, despite scoring 68 goals, 92 assists and 235 minutes in penalties (clear proof that he could take care of himself on the ice) before finally giving him a chance in the NHL.

The NHL is a sport for big men. There have been players who were small in stature, but they were usually goaltenders, and any short player who made it never really lasted that long. But it seems strange that the Flames had any trepidation about Fleury's size, especially after an incident at the 1987 Junior World Championships where he started a brawl with the Russian players that led to both teams being thrown out of the tournament. (Fleury was just defending his teammate Everett Sanipass, who was being attacked by a Russian player.) Yet, still with some skepticism, the Flames finally called Fleury up mid-season, and he proved all the naysayers wrong straight from the start.

In the 36 remaining games of the regular season, Fleury scored 14 goals in 36 games. Calgary fans quickly grew attached to the speedy little forward with quick feet and even quicker hands. Those skills came in handy in the playoffs as the Flames progressed through the preliminary rounds and then into the finals versus a tough Montreal Canadiens squad. It was a battle of goaltenders as Mike Vernon outshone the Canadiens Patrick Roy, and Flames defenseman Al McInnis put in the performance of his career to secure the Flames' first franchise Stanley Cup. Theoren Fleury, the rookie no one wanted to take a chance on, had his first Stanley Cup.

Fleury continued season after season to prove to all those who thought he could not make it in the NHL that not only could he play there, but that he could also be one of the best. He achieved the magic number of 51 goals in the 1990–91 season and was selected to the NHL All-Star team. Three years later he was named captain of the Calgary Flames and established himself as one of the league's top snipers. In the late 1990s, players were not scoring that many points because of the overwhelming defensive style at the time, but Fleury was consistently in the league's top 20 in scoring.

Throughout his time with the Flames, he was one of the best players, and when he was eligible for free agency and it came time to sign him, the Flames simply did not have the money to keep him on the team. So at the March deadline of the 1998–99 season, Fleury said goodbye to his beloved Calgary and took up residence with the Colorado Avalanche.

The Avalanche management was looking for a veteran player with playoff experience to help the team through the playoffs. Theoren Fleury was a help to the Avalanche but not enough to get them to the Stanley Cup finals; they lost in the Conference finals to the Dallas Stars. It was a short stay in Colorado, as Fleury was moved to the New York Rangers for the start of the 1999–2000 season. After a sluggish first year with the Rangers, with only 15 goals, the old Theoren Fleury returned to form, scoring 30 goals and 44 assists. But after more than a decade in the NHL, Fleury was starting to wind down, and the Rangers sensed it was time to move him to another team after the 2001–02 season. He landed in Chicago, a city that would not be good for Fleury, both personally and professionally.

Fleury, who had always battled alcohol addiction throughout his career, was handed a 25-game suspension for his abuse and placed in an NHL recovery program. Upon his return to the league, fans in opposing arenas were less than kind and taunted Fleury every time he hit the ice. Just after he returned to the Hawks, he missed a practice and was suspended for two games. Fleury had claimed it was a faulty alarm clock that was responsible, but given his history of alcoholism, few believed his version of events.

Things got worse around the middle of the 2002–03 season when he got involved in an incident at a Columbus, Ohio strip club. Fleury does not really remember what happened that night, but apparently he had been throwing dollar bills at some women when for some unknown reason a bouncer knocked Fleury out cold. Two of Fleury's teammates came to his rescue and asked the local police to get them out of the club. What exactly happened that night probably will never be known, but the incident was the final straw for the Hawks, and Fleury never made it back to the NHL.

After getting some more help for his alcohol problem, he still wanted to play hockey. Playing in any of the North American leagues seemed out of the question because of Fleury's history, so he traveled to Ireland to play for the Belfast Giants of the British Elite Ice Hockey League. He started off with a bang, scoring a hat trick as well as helping out with four assists in his opening game, but things quickly soured when Fleury's temper got the best of him in one game.

During that game, while serving out a penalty in the box, a drunk fan took it upon himself to taunt Fleury mercilessly from the stands. It was at that point that Fleury tried to climb over the glass to get at the fan. He then directed his anger at the officials of the game and later said that he would never play in the league again. Fleury's European vacation only lasted 34 games, but he did score 22 goals.

Since retiring from hockey, Fleury has calmed his inner beast and now is happily married, living in Calgary where he runs a concrete business with his brother. Fleury admits that he made many mistakes during his career but that it was one heck of a ride.

Stats

Season	Team	Games Played	Goals	Assists	Points	Penalties
1988–89	Calgary Flames	36	14	20	34	46
1989–90	Calgary Flames	80	31	35	66	157
1990–91	Calgary Flames	79	51	53	104	136
1991–92	Calgary Flames	80	33	40	73	133
1992–93	Calgary Flames	83	34	66	100	88
1993–94	Calgary Flames	83	40	45	85	186
1994–95	Calgary Flames	47	29	29	58	112
1995–96	Calgary Flames	80	46	50	96	112
1996–97	Calgary Flames	81	29	38	67	104
1997–98	Calgary Flames	82	27	51	78	197
1998–99	Calgary Flames	60	30	39	69	68
	Colorado Avalanche	15	10	14	24	18
1999–2000	New York Rangers	80	15	49	64	68
2000–01	New York Rangers	62	30	44	74	122
2001–02	New York Rangers	82	24	39	63	216
2002–03	Chicago Blackhawks	54	12	21	33	77
NHL Totals		1084	455	633	1088	1840

Grant
Fuhr

Born in Spruce Grove, Alberta, on September 28, 1962, Grant Fuhr had a rough start in life. A child of unmarried teenagers, his father was black and his mother part Cree, Fuhr was given up for adoption and raised by a foster family. Despite not knowing who his birth parents were, Fuhr blossomed under the care of his adoptive family and was encouraged early on to take up an interest in sports.

Naturally, as a boy growing up in rural Canada, hockey was everywhere, but Fuhr was also quite the baseball player. His fielding position of choice should be of no surprise; he was a catcher. He was so good that the Pittsburgh Pirates even offered him an opportunity to make it into the majors, but he passed that up to concentrate on his future in hockey.

Goaltending was Fuhr's passion. He was the kind of athlete who thrived under pressure, and when the game is on the line, there is no more pressure-filled position than that of the goaltender.

At 17, Fuhr was good enough to join the Victoria Cougars of the Western Hockey League and became their number-one goaltender. In his first season with the Cougars he won 30 games and lost only 12. In his second season he followed that up with 48 wins and nine losses. He was proving to be a clutch goaltender who could always be relied on to get his team out of any jam. His athleticism was by far one of his most impressive attributes. He had a reaction time like no other, and hand-eye coordination that was responsible for many jaw-dropping miraculous saves. It was no surprise then that the Edmonton Oilers selected him eighth overall at the 1981 NHL Entry Draft and immediately put him to work for the 1981–82 season at only 18 years old.

Fuhr joined the Oilers just when they were starting to become the team of the mid-1980s. Before Fuhr came along, the Oilers had relied on the services of goaltender Andy Moog, and though Moog was a good player, he never seemed to take the team to the next level required to win a Stanley Cup; for that you needed a great goaltender. Fuhr was that goalie.

"He had a rare ability to give up three or four goals in an 8–4 game, and then when the team needed him to shut down momentum, he could do that," said former NHL goaltender Darren Pang in the book *Without Fear,* by Kevin Allen and Bob Duff.

Fuhr never really had great goals-against averages (neither did any other goaltender during the '80s for that matter) because at the time, hockey was a more open affair with less focus on the defensive. It was called "firewagon" hockey and was a style perfected by Wayne Gretzky and the Oilers, but they could afford to keep the focus on scoring goals because they knew they could rely on Fuhr at the other end.

"The Oilers used to give up as many great scoring chances as any team in the league," said former NHL coach Jacques Demers. "The credit always went to Wayne Gretzky, Mark Messier, Glenn Anderson, Jari Kurri and company, but Grant Fuhr knew every night that shots were going to come from everywhere. He never got enough credit."

After two years with the Oilers and sharing goaltending duties with Andy Moog, Fuhr struggled in net for a time and was spent back down to the minors for conditioning. When he returned for the 1983–84 season, the Oilers got the goaltender they had wanted when they originally drafted him in 1981. He was stellar during the regular season, but it was for the playoffs that Fuhr saved his best stuff.

The Oilers were looking for a little redemption after failing to beat the New York Islanders in the previous season's Stanley Cup finals. They had proven during the regular season that they were one of the best teams in the league—they had the top scoring lines in NHL history and had one of the game's premiere young goalies in net. All they had left to prove was that they could win.

Edmonton easily made it through the division semi-finals against the Winnipeg Jets, but then they ran up against their provincial rivals the Calgary Flames in the division finals. It was in this series that they proved just what kind of team they were, and it was where the name Grant Fuhr truly established itself.

During the regular season the Flames had finished second in the Oilers division but were lengths behind in terms of scoring power. It seemed like the series would be a cakewalk for the highly skilled Oilers squad, but the Flames always played with a little extra passion when taking on their rivals. For Edmonton, a team that scored 446 goals during the regular season, the series was a rather low-scoring affair and ended up being a battle between Fuhr and the Flames' goaltender Rejean Lemelin. The series went to seven games after Fuhr gave up an overtime goal in game six, but the Oilers and Fuhr shut the Flames down in the final game to advance deeper into the playoffs. After knocking off the Minnesota North Stars in four straight games, the Oilers were once again back in the Stanley Cup finals against the New York Islanders. But this time they were ready, and so was Grant Fuhr.

Game one was an uncharacteristically low-scoring game with the Oilers only managing one goal and Fuhr getting the shutout. While the Islanders did manage to pepper six goals past him and take the second game, the Oilers won the next three straight and took home their first Stanley Cup.

The key to Fuhr's success in goal for the Oilers was that he was always calm and unflappable in net. Goaltenders as a species are known to be a little strange. Most have intense preparations before a game and can be moody and reclusive. (Hall of Fame goaltender Glenn Hall used to throw up before every game.) But Fuhr was always calm and relaxed before a game, and when possible, he always tried to get in a game of golf before playing in net because he said it eased his mind.

On the ice, things could not have gone any better for Fuhr and the Oilers. He backstopped them to another Stanley Cup in 1985, got burned by the Flames in 1986, was eliminated from the playoffs after his own defenseman Steve Smith scored the game- and series-deciding goal on him, and won another Cup in 1987, 1988, and in 1990. Fuhr also appeared in six All-Star games and took home the Vezina Trophy as the NHL's top goaltender in 1988.

But off the ice things always seemed to go wrong for Fuhr.

He was married and divorced twice during the '80s, but a more difficult issue was his drug problem. It was no secret to many on his team that Fuhr was addicted to cocaine. It wasn't a real problem until around 1989 and 1990 when the league got wind of his habit and suspended him for 60 games for using drugs. The suspension was the necessary tough love Fuhr needed to get his life back on track. It wasn't easy for him, though. His habit had used up a lot of the money he had earned as an NHL player, and now that he wasn't working he was in severe financial difficulty. But he sought treatment and in 1990 checked himself into the Betty Ford Clinic to get the professional help he needed. Used to making saves on the ice, he finally saved himself from an uncertain future.

"My biggest problem was I wanted to be the way I was in school, just a normal guy. But people didn't look at me like I was just another guy on the street and I had a problem dealing with it. Drug use was an escape to get away. I used to run and hide from problems. I led a double life," Fuhr told a reporter from the *Edmonton Journal.*

After cleaning himself up, Fuhr returned to the Oilers lineup in time for the end of the 1990–91 season and the start of the playoffs. He was back to his old ways in the playoffs, helping the Oilers get past some tough teams to get to the Conference finals. He helped beat a strong Calgary squad in the first round and was solid through four overtime games against his old teammate Wayne Gretzky and his Los Angeles Kings in the second round, but unfortunately Fuhr could not stop everything in the Conference finals, and the Oilers were eliminated by the Minnesota North Stars.

After the disappointing loss in the playoffs, the Oilers needed to dump some expensive salaries, so they traded Fuhr along with Glenn Anderson and Craig Berube to the Toronto Maple Leafs. Toronto wasn't the greatest fit for the veteran goaltender, and his once stellar numbers began to decline. Although it wasn't all his doing—after all, the Leafs were not the greatest of teams—Fuhr was just not what the Leafs needed. That was made all the more clear when young rookie goaltender Felix Potvin joined the team and helped turn the Leafs around. Fuhr was relegated to the role of second-string goaltender and wasn't happy in his new position. He was then bounced around to the Buffalo Sabres and the Los Angeles Kings over the next few years before finally landing with the St. Louis Blues.

It was with the Blues that Fuhr had a rebirth of sorts. He was reunited with his old teammates, Wayne Gretzky, Glenn Anderson, Charlie Huddy and Esa Tikkanen, and had a record year as the Blues' number-one goaltender. In that 1995–96 season, Fuhr started in a record 79 games, the most by any goaltender in NHL history.

Over the next few seasons he continued as the Blues' top goaltender, but by the 1998–99 season the old-timer was starting to slow down. In 1999–2000 the Calgary Flames signed him as a free agent, but Fuhr only played 23 games with the team. At the end of that season he decided to hang up his pads and leave the goaltending to the younger guys.

However, he did not stay away from hockey completely. Fuhr joined up with the Prince George Cougars of the Western Hockey League as their goalie coach and eventually got the call from an old friend of his to join him in Phoenix to be their goalie coach. Part owner and head coach of the Phoenix Coyotes, Wayne Gretzky knew that Fuhr would make an excellent addition to his coaching staff, and that Fuhr would always have something to teach after having gone through so much in life.

In November 2003 Fuhr received the ultimate honor for his career in hockey when he was inducted into the Hockey Hall of Fame. Only a month earlier in a ceremony that meant so much to Fuhr, the Edmonton Oilers officially retired his number to the rafters. It is an honor not given to many players, especially from a group that was so filled with talent as the Oilers. The tears on Fuhr's face during the ceremony showed just how much the tribute meant to him.

Stats

Season	Team	Games Played	Minutes Played	Goals Against	Shut out	Goals Against Average	Wins	Losses	Ties
1981–82	Edmonton Oilers	48	2847	157	0	3.31	28	5	14
1982–83	Edmonton Oilers	32	1803	129	0	4.29	13	12	5
1983–84	Edmonton Oilers	45	2625	171	1	3.91	30	10	4
1984–85	Edmonton Oilers	46	2559	165	1	3.87	26	8	7
1985–86	Edmonton Oilers	40	2184	143	0	3.93	29	8	0
1986–87	Edmonton Oilers	44	2388	137	0	3.44	22	13	3
1987–88	Edmonton Oilers	75	4304	246	4	3.43	40	24	9
1988–89	Edmonton Oilers	59	3341	213	1	3.83	23	26	6
1989–90	Edmonton Oilers	21	1081	70	1	3.89	9	7	3
1990–91	Edmonton Oilers	13	778	39	1	3.01	6	4	3
1991–92	Toronto Maple Leafs	66	3774	230	2	3.66	25	33	5
1992–93	Toronto Maple Leafs	29	1665	87	1	3.14	13	9	4
	Buffalo Sabres	29	1694	98	0	3.47	11	15	2
1993–94	Buffalo Sabres	32	1726	106	2	3.68	13	12	3
1994–95	Buffalo Sabres	3	180	12	0	4.00	1	2	0
	Los Angeles Kings	14	698	47	0	4.04	1	7	3

Stats cont'd.

Season	Team	Games Played	Minutes Played	Goals Against	Shut out	Goals Against Average	Wins	Losses	Ties
1995–96	St. Louis Blues	79	4365	209	3	2.87	30	28	16
1996–97	St. Louis Blues	73	4261	193	3	2.72	33	27	11
1997–98	St. Louis Blues	58	3274	138	3	2.53	29	21	6
1998–99	St. Louis Blues	39	2193	89	2	2.44	16	11	8
1999–2000	Calgary Flames	23	1205	77	0	3.83	5	13	2
NHL Totals		868	8945	2756	25	3.38	403	295	114

Top Ten Greatest First Nations Players

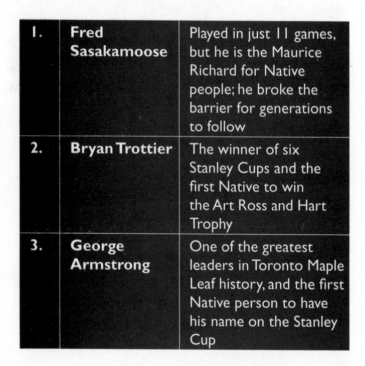

1.	**Fred Sasakamoose**	Played in just 11 games, but he is the Maurice Richard for Native people; he broke the barrier for generations to follow
2.	**Bryan Trottier**	The winner of six Stanley Cups and the first Native to win the Art Ross and Hart Trophy
3.	**George Armstrong**	One of the greatest leaders in Toronto Maple Leaf history, and the first Native person to have his name on the Stanley Cup

4.	Reggie Leach	Stanley Cup winner and prolific scorer
5.	Carey Price	One of the new school of athlete who, although he has only just started, will have a brilliant career
6.	Jonathan Cheechoo	Winner of the Maurice Richard Trophy as the league's top scorer in 2005–06
7.	Sheldon Souray	With his blistering shot, good looks and community work, he is a role model for young people
8.	Theoren Fleury	Despite his history of alcohol abuse and violent outbursts, the diminutive forward made a major impact in the NHL during his time
9.	Ted Nolan	Became the first Native head coach in the NHL
10.	Stan Jonathan	One of the toughest and roughest in league history, and a good player at the same time

Other Players

While a few sources claimed that the players below were of First Nations ancestry, I was unable to verify it.

Cody McCormick

Season	Team	Games Played	Goals	Assists	Points	Penalties
2003–04	Colorado Avalanche	44	2	3	5	73
2005–06	Colorado Avalanche	45	4	4	8	29
2006–07	Colorado Avalanche	6	0	1	1	6
2007–08	Colorado Avalanche	40	2	2	4	50
NHL Totals		135	8	10	18	158